STORIES OF OU

RUM-RUNNING

RUM-RUNNING

ALLISON LAWLOR

NIMBUS
PUBLISHING LTD

Nimbus Publishing Limited
PO Box 9166
Halifax, NS B3K 5M8
(902) 455-4286
www.nimbus.ca

Printed and bound in Canada

Design: Aaron Harpell, Hammerhead Design, Halifax, NS
Author photo: Robbie Frame

Library and Archives Canada Cataloguing in Publication

Lawlor, Allison, 1971-
Rum-running / Allison Lawlor.
(Stories of our past) Includes bibliographical references and index. ISBN 978-1-55109-734-3

1. Smuggling—Atlantic Provinces—History. 2. Prohibition—Atlantic Provinces—History. I. Title. II. Series: Stories of our past (Halifax, N.S.)

HV5091.C3L39 2009   364.1'33   C2009-903373-9

We acknowledge the financial support of the Government of Canada through the Book Publishing Industry Development Program (BPIDP) and the Canada Council, and of the Province of Nova Scotia through the Department of Tourism, Culture and Heritage for our publishing activities.

Contents

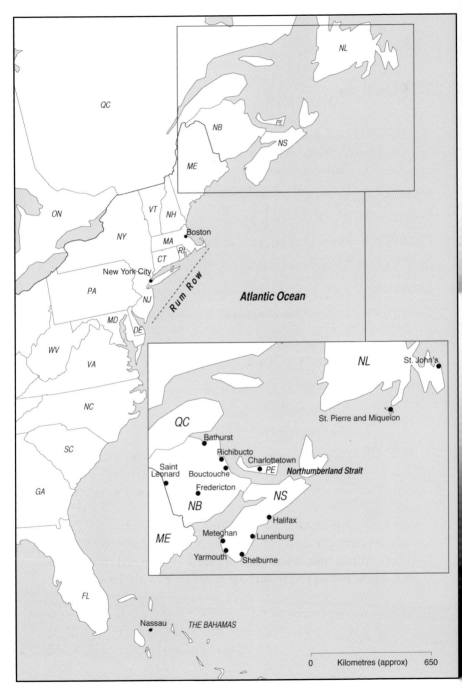

The areas where rum-runners operated on the Atlantic Coast

Rum Row

Maritime rum-runners picked up liquor in St. Pierre and Mique-lon, French islands off the coast of Newfoundland, and delivered it to "Rum Row," a line or run of ships that anchored off the coast to off-load their cargoes of liquor. Most often these deliveries took place off the coast of Massachusetts, New York, or New Jersey, but sometimes they were as far south as Florida. There it was loaded onto smaller, faster contact boats in international waters just outside the twelve-mile jurisdictional limit. The contact boats then brought the liquor into the United States, where it was distributed by criminal organizations.

It is probably not an exaggeration to say that during Prohibition in the United States, rum-runners—often enterprising Maritimers—landed liquor on virtually every mile of inland shore from the Virginia Capes to Maine.

❝ For a long time newspapers featured operations of Rum Row. Ships with valuable cargoes of choice liquors hovered or lurked beyond coastal waters, to supply bootleggers who could run the blockades along our shores. The most notorious Rum Rows were off the coasts of New Jersey and Florida. Cities along the eastern seaboard received practically their entire supply of foreign liquor from such sources. At one time it was quite apparent that no real effort was being made to put an end to such open defiance of our laws. ❞

—Mabel Walker Willebrandt, the assistant attorney-general in charge of Prohibition enforcement in the U.S., 1922–1929 (from The Inside of Prohibition, *1929)*

Introduction

Few other times in Atlantic Canadian history have been the subject of more speculation, more disputes, and more folklore than the Prohibition years.

In the early 1920s, fishermen started trading their cargoes of cod for crate-loads of liquor to bring to their dry American neighbours. The telling and re-telling of stories of these smugglers, who faced pirates and dangerous chases on the sea, evolved into Maritime folklore about the rum-running trade.

Rum-running came at the perfect time for small fishing villages across the Maritimes. In the ten years following the end of World War One, fish prices in Lunenburg County, Nova Scotia, plummeted. As a result, the number of vessels fishing out of the county dropped from a high of 149 to a low of 84 in 1927, and incomes

The term **"rum-runner"** was probably coined in the Maritimes, since rum was the most popular drink there, especially in fishing communities. Americans preferred drinks such as Scotch and whisky, so Maritimers actually transported much more Scotch than rum to their thirsty neighbours to the south.

" The big boats—the mother ships—they generally would lay off fifteen to twenty miles, sometimes fifty miles they'd be laying off there. You couldn't do anything about them. No, nothing. Just stand by them. Lay off. We knew they were there, see them all the time. Night time, you put the searchlights on them. Those big fellows anchored off, they're only warehouses—floating warehouses. And these speedboats—we called them speedboats—they run out from land, load and come in, make a landing. Maybe forty to fifty kegs at a time—three hundred cases, whatever. We seized quite a few of them. But a lot would get in. You can't watch it all you know. You'd get two or three different fellows to load that night. You don't know which one to call. There was always a decoy to draw you away. They weren't fools you know. They had tricks. They'd reverse their sidelights. You'd think they were going opposite of you. But we had big searchlights. Then they put smokescreens up—come out of their exhaust. They had things to put on the exhaust, old oil and stuff and one mass of smoke, just fog all around—but we'd find them after. But they'd get clear. It's all get clear. The big warehouse would be empty and away he'd go. Oh, it was quite a game, boy. A lot of fun in it. "

—As told by Milton MacKenzie, who worked on the Canadian Preventive Service cutters Fleur de Lis *and* Louisbourg, *to* Cape Breton Magazine *in 1975.*

earned from fishing fell by more than half, leading many local fishers to turn to the rum trade, which was much more profitable. In January 1925, the *Maritime Merchant* reported that about half of the Lunenburg fishing fleet of close to 100 vessels was engaged in the rum trade. Many of these boats were leased to American crime syndicates at the rate of $2,500 per month. Rum-running was pervasive. Before long, everyone in the Maritimes was either involved in rum-running or knew someone who participated in the lucrative activity.

Lunenburg Harbour in the 1930s

Despite strong opposition from some church groups, many coastal communities wouldn't have survived without the rum-running trade. Aside from steady wages, it also provided a lot of work for local shipbuilders. Soon after the beginning of the rum trade, shipyards were busy with orders for boats designed specifically for rum-running. Most of the boats built for rum-running came from shipyards in southwest Nova Scotia, but other Maritime shipyards occasionally took part in the trade, as well.

The Maritime provinces were perfectly located to supply booze to their American neighbours. One of the most popular routes to get liquor into the United States was a channel from the rugged islands of St. Pierre and Miquelon to Rum Row off New York. Nova Scotian captains and schooners were the principal operators along this route, loading West Indian rum, British gin, French champagne, and Canadian whisky onto their boats from the warehouses lining St. Pierre's waterfront and delivering it to Rum Row. Most of this liquor was bound for agents of notorious gangsters like Al Capone, who waited in New York for delivery of the contraband to sell to clients willing to pay a hefty price for a bottle of banned liquor, but some of the liquor from St. Pierre ended up in Canada, as well.

When Prohibition ended in the United States in 1933, demand for smuggled alcohol dropped and soon the rum-runners were out of business. A web of silence fell over the activities of those involved in the illicit trade. Few wanted to talk about that time in Maritime history because of shame and denial. Many

The *Silver Arrow*, a rum-running boat built by M. E. Leary in Dayspring, Nova Scotia, in 1929

THE RUM-RUNNING BUSINESS

While many argue that there was nothing romantic about the Prohibition era—that it was simply a time when people were driven by greed to break the law and exploit others' weaknesses for alcohol—it is hard not to be fascinated by the tall tales of adventurous and enterprising rum-runners. Bill McCoy, probably the most famous American rum-runner of his time, described what it was like to arrive with a shipload of booze on Rum Row, near New York, in early 1923:

> I used to look at that long line of craft, anchored all the way from Montauk to Cape May, with the pride a first settler would feel in the growth of his town....
>
> Schooners and yachts, wind jamming square-riggers from Scandinavia, tramps from England and Germany, converted tugs and submarine chasers, anything with a bottom that would float and a hold that could be filled with booze, they stretched away in a long line, bowing to the surges, swinging with the tide and wind, waiting in apathy all day for the strenuous activity that began as soon as night fell. Up and down that long line white cutters plodded, surveying the old-timers, inspecting new arrivals. Dories floundered across from ship to ship as the captains and crews of the fleet exchanged visits. It was a roaring, boisterous, sinful-and-glad-of-it marine Main street of shifting membership and continually increasing size, and I was its founder and first citizen.
>
> My reputation was all the advertisement I needed. Until the cutters began to be annoying I sold my liquor almost as fast as we could bring it up from the hold. One night that summer [1923], when the sea was calm and all America apparently wanted a drink, I set the Rum Row record by unloading into small craft 3,400 cases between 5 and 10 PM. I could have sold twice as much that night if I had had it, but they cleaned me out, and at 10 we sailed back to Nassau for more.

wanted to put the era behind them. But by the 1980s, there was a realization that a part of history was dying and would be forgotten if the silence continued. People started talking more openly and telling their stories, and this controversial and colourful chapter of Atlantic Canadian history was reopened.

RUM

Rum bottles

Rum is thought to have originated on West Indian plantations sometime during the sixteenth century. In an elemental form, it consisted of little more than a naturally produced beer fermented by yeast spores settling on pools of uncrystallized cane juice and molasses discarded from sugar mills. The first regular importation of rum in the region began around 1670 through New England trade with Newfoundland.

CHAPTER 1

PROHIBITION ON BOTH SIDES OF THE BORDER

CALLED "the noble experiment" by American president Herbert Hoover, Prohibition became law in the United States on January 16, 1920, under what was known as the Volstead Act. When that happened, the general use of alcohol was outlawed across the country.

Prohibition: The outlaw of the general use of alcohol, making it illegal to manufacture, sell, or transport liquor. Prohibition was in effect in parts of the United States and Canada between 1916 and 1948.

Lawmakers greatly underestimated the American people's desire for alcohol and didn't anticipate the explosion of organized crime that followed. Prohibition proved to be a wild time, when criminals in the United States not only controlled the liquor business, but expanded into other areas of crime and corruption. Gangs spread across the country, corruption escalated, and law enforcement agencies were overwhelmed.

Millions of normally law-abiding citizens began breaking the law, lured by the prospect of making a quick buck during tough financial times. The Volstead Act, otherwise known as the National Prohibition Act, enabled the United States government to enforce the Eighteenth Amendment to the Constitution. The amendment itself did not ban the actual consumption of alcohol, but made buying it legally difficult. The amendment, along with the Volstead Act, prohibited the manufacture, sale, or transportation of alcoholic beverages. Americans soon found ways to get around the law. They quickly established supply routes along the coasts for receiving imported alcoholic beverages and created illegal manufacturing facilities.

THE VOLSTEAD ACT

Named after Congressman Andrew J. Volstead, a Minnesota Republican, the Volstead Act was the enabling legislation for the enforcement of national Prohibition beginning in 1920 and ending in 1933. It placed a ban on the manufacture, sale, and transportation of all intoxicating beverages in the United States.

THE CANADIAN WAY

PROHIBITION in Canada was more complicated. Prohibition in Canada only outlawed the sale and consumption of alcohol. Even when you couldn't sell liquor in Canada, you could still manufacture and export it. So distilleries in Ontario and Quebec went on producing alcohol that inevitably found its way to the United States.

Under Canadian law, liquor legally produced in or imported into Canada could be exported legally to the United States. The business only became illegal when the rum-runners entered American-controlled waters. The only sanction the Canadian government exercised over this questionable commerce was to charge a validation tax (which ran at nineteen dollars a case) for issuing federal export licences, which was seen as a revenue-producing scheme rather than an attempt at policing the trade. All a rum-runner had to do to obtain an export license was state an improbable destination for his shipment—such as Peru or Panama—and it would be freely waved through Canadian customs. In the spring of 1923, the U.S. State Department asked Canada to refuse licences to ships with cargoes of liquor that were known to be destined for American ports. Initially, the Canadian government dismissed the request, arguing that rum-running did not break any Canadian laws. But after several years of U.S. lobbying, the Canadian government realized that it would have to pay heed to the Americans' request because Canada was providing both an operating base and the raw materials for a multi-billion-dollar criminal industry in the United States. The Canadian and U.S. governments made agreements to shut down most of that traffic. When that happened, distillers in Canada turned to offshore bases, like St. Pierre, where they could, once again, legally export their products.

> Humorist Stephen Leacock described a Prohibitionist as a drunkard who could always be relied on to vote in favour of Prohibition while "in a mood of sentimental remorse."

PROHIBITION BY PROVINCE

Except for a national ban imposed during World War One, each province enacted and repealed Prohibition at different times. Prince Edward Island was the first province in Canada to enact Prohibition, in 1901. The remaining provinces, as well as the Yukon and Newfoundland, followed during World

War One. In March 1918, the Canadian government passed nationwide legislation that would stop the manufacture and importation of liquor into provinces where purchasing it was illegal. However, a loophole in the legislation exempted alcohol for medicinal purposes, resulting in a flood of prescriptions for alcohol. Humorist Stephen Leacock joked about the never-ending lineups at pharmacies with people faking illnesses.

The Canadian government repealed its wartime liquor legislation when the war ended. For the most part, Prohibition in the provinces didn't last for much longer. Quebec rejected it as early as 1919. British Columbia voted "wet" the following year, and soon after, some alcoholic beverages were legally sold there and in the Yukon through government stores. Manitoba inaugurated a system of government sale and control in 1923, followed by Alberta and Saskatchewan in 1924, Newfoundland in 1925, Ontario and New Brunswick in 1927, and Nova Scotia in 1930. The last bastion, Prince Edward Island, held on to Prohibition until 1948.

Nova Scotia Goes Dry With Over Forty Thousand Majority.

Light Vote is Polled in Many Districts Throughout the Province, Ballots Have Proved Beyond Doubt That Nova Scotians Favor Bone-Dry Province.

A headline from the October 27, 1920, edition of the *Lunenburg Progress-Enterprise* announcing Prohibition in Nova Scotia

THE TEMPERANCE MOVEMENT

Long before prohibitive legislation was passed in the Maritime provinces, the anti-liquor temperance forces were at work. Temperance activity in the region dates back to 1793, when a group of Hants County farmers in Nova Scotia met to form the Association Against Spiritous Liquors. They agreed to abandon the practice of paying their workers in rum, and in doing so expressed their concern over "the excessive use of spirituous liquors among the labouring poor."

The Temperance Hall in Sherbrooke Village, Nova Scotia

THE GREAT

TEMPERANCE DRINKS

LYMAN'S FLUID COFFEE

CONCENTRATED

LYMAN'S

EXTRACT OF

COFFEE.

FOR TRAVELLING.
FOR STAYING AT HOME.
FOR THE SEASIDE.
FOR PIC-NICKING.
FOR CAMPING OUT.
THE GREAT CONVENIENCE AND LUXURY OF THE DAY.

RICH AND FULL FLAVORED, WHOLESOME, STIMULATING, EASY OF USE, ECONOMICAL, THE GENERAL FAVORITE, NO CHEAP SUBSTITUTE OF PEAS, WHEAT OR BARLEY, BUT GENUINE MOCHA AND OLD GOVERNMENT JAVA.

Can be served up, PIPING HOT, in A MOMENT.

DOMINICA LIME FRUIT JUICE.

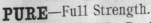

PURE—Full Strength.
WHOLESOME—Purifies the Blood.
REFRESHING—An Agreeable Tonic.
COOLING } Just the thing for the Hot Weather.

ABSOLUTELY FREE FROM ALCOHOL.

For Sale by Grocers and Druggists in Pints and Quarts (Imperial Measure.)

REFINED EXPRESSLY FOR

LYMAN, SONS & CO., MONTREAL.

A Liberal Discount to the Trade.

Read Advertisement of Dominion Line Steamers, next page.

An 1885 advertisement for temperance drinks

Across the Maritimes, temperance societies were soon formed to "reform the wicked" and end the use of alcohol. Supporters of the temperance movement weren't just

Temperance: a total or partial abstinence from drinking alcohol

religious fanatics, but responsible people reacting to what they saw as a social illness. Rum was everywhere at the time. In his history of Pictou County, Nova Scotia, Reverend George Patterson recalled,

> A member of my congregation told me of himself and others working at a job for a fortnight in the heat of summer drinking each their quart bottle of rum a day, and not at the time feeling the worse of it, though they felt unfit for work of any sort for the following week or two. Men would sometimes drink half a pint at a time, or even a pint, and I knew of one who undertook to drink a whole quart at a time, and did so, but it nearly cost him his life.

A LOSING BATTLE

Not long after Prohibition came into effect, the impossibility of enforcing it became apparent. Bootleggers and smugglers were better equipped and better financed than law officials in both Canada and the United States. And aside from supplying liquor to Americans, ports up and down the East Coast of Canada were also busy with midnight runs of liquor coming ashore.

When Prohibition hit cities like Halifax, "blind pigs"—establishments that surreptitiously sold alcoholic beverages—sprouted up everywhere. In an interview in 1987, Alex Nickerson, a former newspaperman, recalled how one infamous bootlegging family ran their illegal operation:

This Dauphinee family were famous bootleggers. They ran booze in from Sambro and the mouth of the Northwest Arm and there was a whole bunch of them. Right in the middle of downtown, they had an old frame house with iron doors, and when you went in, you walked upstairs for your shot of beer or rum. They were always being raided. They built a lookout. It projected from the front of the house, upstairs, and the fellow on duty could look up and down the street, and if he saw the police coming, he would give a warning. By the time the law got through the metal doors the rum was flushed down the toilet.

Bootleggers—not just in Halifax, but throughout Nova Scotia—were known for their ingenuity in hiding liquor. While demolishing a building on Water Street in Halifax in the 1930s, a wrecking crew found a sink inside the front door. A hidden pipeline ran through the house, up a backyard slope, and into another building on Hollis Street, which runs parallel to Water Street. "The bootlegger on Water Street could turn a tap on," Nickerson said, "and rum would come down the pipe from Hollis and into a pitcher in the sink. But he could also shut it off and turn another valve, and then out came only water."

In Halifax, drunkenness remained the most prevalent offence throughout the 1920s despite Prohibition in the province. On November 19, 1929, one of the largest police court dockets in years shows twenty-nine prisoners gathered over the weekend, most for drunkenness.

In 1929, a plebiscite was held on Prohibition in Nova Scotia. Those in favour of repealing the act argued that government control of the sale of liquor would generate the revenue needed to help pay for social programs such as old-age pensions. The province voted for government control of the sale of alcohol, and the Liquor Control Act of 1930 was passed under Conservative premier Edgar Nelson Rhodes. By August of that year, the first

BOLD GANG OF ROBBERS TAKES 3 TRUCKLOADS OF RUM FROM CUSTOMS HOUSE

Twenty Armed Men Take Part In Daring Robbery In Early Morning At Parrsboro And In Five Autos Convoy Three Truckloads Of Rum Away From Town, After Driving Caretaker And Citizens To Cover

The headline from a November 21, 1925, article in the *Halifax Morning Chronicle* describing a daring liquor robbery in Parrsboro, Nova Scotia

liquor stores in the province were opened for business—three in Halifax and one in Dartmouth.

When Prohibition ended both in Canada and the United States, the general feeling was that the Prohibitionists' "cure" for what they believed to be the social problems of the time was worse than the disease.

CHAPTER 2

THE REAL MCCOY

Standing six-feet-two, with broad shoulders and a voice resembling a foghorn, New York-born Bill McCoy was probably the most famous rum-runner of his time. To some he was a folk hero, smuggling booze under the noses of corrupt law officials to supply the needs of everyday, common folks. Dubbed the founder of Rum Row, he claimed to have been lured into rum-running by the money to be made, but to have stayed for the thrill of it. A self-proclaimed teetotaller (a person who doesn't drink alcohol), he wasn't there for his love of rum.

Most famous as the captain of a fishing schooner named *Tomoka*, McCoy sold between fourteen and twenty thousand gallons of

> During a calm clear night Rum Row sounded like a motorboat regatta. The darkness shook to the sound of engines rattling and booming. The craft all, naturally, ran without lights, and now and again cut each other down.
>
> —*Captain Bill McCoy*

liquor (the average swimming pool holds twenty-five thousand gallons of water) over his four years as a rum-runner. Despite being called a rum-runner, he mostly ran Scotch and rye.

McCoy quickly earned the reputation of providing customers with quality products. He never cut his liquor or watered it down, and some say the expression "It's the real McCoy" refers to the quality of McCoy's booze. While he may not have cut his liquor, those who bought it certainly did. Practically all of it was cut four times by purchasers who diluted and fortified it with grain alcohol before it was sold.

McCoy is credited with the idea of bringing large ships to the edge of the three-mile limit of U.S. jurisdiction. From there he would sell his liquor to local fishermen and captains of what became known as "contact boats"—smaller, faster boats that could more easily outrun Coast Guard ships, and could dock in any cove to transfer their goods to a waiting truck. Before long, other rum-runners were following this

Captain Bill McCoy

pattern; soon the three-mile limit became known as the "Rum Line" and the line of ships waiting was called "Rum Row." In 1924, the U.S. Congress expanded the three-mile limit to a twelve-mile limit, which made it harder for the smaller boats to make the trip.

Aside from Rum Row, McCoy is also said to have been the first to recognize the French islands of St. Pierre and Miquelon off the coast of Newfoundland—which were not subject to the same Prohibition laws as Canada and the United States—as the ideal location for warehousing liquor.

Before he got into rum-running, McCoy lived a relatively quiet life. Born in Syracuse, New York, in 1877, McCoy moved to Florida with his family in 1900. Shortly thereafter, he and his brother Ben began building boats on the banks of Florida's Halifax River. In 1920, with the boat-building business struggling and Prohibition coming into effect, the owner of a schooner named *Dorothy W* approached Mc-Coy with a proposition. The man had a contract to carry a load of rye whisky from Nassau to Atlantic City and needed a skipper to sail his boat. He offered McCoy one

BURLOCKS

Bill McCoy was frustrated with the money he was losing from glass liquor bottles getting smashed as they were loaded into his ship, so he designed what he called a "burlock." This was a package of six bottles padded with straw, arranged in a pyramid formation, and tightly sewn into burlap bags. Not only did they take up less space than wooden crates and barrels, but the bags could also be tossed around without breaking the glass. If the burlocks had to be thrown overboard during a raid, they sank quickly to the bottom of the sea (unlike wooden crates, which bobbed in the water for weeks). The U.S. Coast Guard soon began referring to these sacks as "hams."

hundred dollars a day to take the position. McCoy was tempted by the offer, but turned it down. Instead, he and his brother decided to go into the smuggling business on their own. Later that year, McCoy travelled to Gloucester, Massachusetts, in search of a suitable boat. There he found the *Henry L. Marshall*, a ninety-foot fishing schooner built of white oak, which could carry fifteen hundred cases of liquor in crates or three thousand cases in burlap bags. He bought the schooner for twenty thousand dollars.

The *Arethusa*, later renamed *Tomoka*, a rum-runner owned by Bill McCoy

In early 1921, McCoy set sail for Nassau, which for the next four years would be his home port. Even before he had time to anchor in Nassau, an entrepreneur approached him with an offer to pay him ten dollars per case if he delivered fifteen hundred cases of liquor to Savannah. McCoy agreed, battling gales and steering clear of the authorities to successfully deliver the liquor. Upon his return to Nassau about a week later, he banked fifteen thousand dollars for the job.

Later that year, McCoy returned to Gloucester to buy a better boat to replace the *Henry L. Marshall*. He found one, and because the boat's owners were bankrupt, it was on sale for only twenty-one thousand dollars. McCoy paid cash. He considered the boat, which he named *Arethusa*, the finest of the Gloucester-built fishing schooners. Now that he had the *Arethusa*, McCoy decided that instead of selling the *Henry L. Marshall*, he would hire it out, as he could make more money owning two boats.

In late July 1921, McCoy anchored his beloved *Arethusa* off Long Island. The boat was loaded with five thousand cases of liquor, two thousand of which were consigned to gangster-type operators. The remainder was "first come, first serve" to any customer who came to him with enough money. *Arethusa* hovered in the waters off Long Island for a week, and during this time McCoy made fifty thousand dollars.

After this successful venture, McCoy returned to Nassau and worked out a system to avoid the scrutiny of authorities—he would clear customs in Nassau with a load of cargo bound for Halifax, where it was still legal to import and export liquor. He figured this would be safe because he wasn't going to the United States.

For the most part, this system worked. But on one occasion, after returning to Nassau, the authorities looked at his papers and expressed their suspicion. "You never went to Halifax," they accused.

"No," McCoy answered. "I had an opportunity to sell my cargo on the high seas."

"You can't do that."

"I did do it."

"But it's not legal."

"Show me," McCoy demanded, "any law that says a master can't clear for a port, discharge on the high seas, and return to his home port, providing he has touched nowhere else meanwhile." They tried to find one, but there was no law stating that this wasn't legal. And so McCoy would continue to clear for Halifax without ever getting there. On his return, he would swear an affidavit that the cargo was sold at sea and had touched no port, which satisfied the Nassau customs officers.

The pattern set by McCoy caught on rapidly. Within a few months, several rum ships were working in this manner on the waterways from Maine to Florida, with the majority off the coast of Boston, New York, Norfolk, and Savannah.

DISCOVERING ST. PIERRE

ONE day in 1921, the *Arethusa*, loaded with a shipment of liquor from Nassau and captained by a hired man, was damaged at sea. The captain anchored the boat off the Nova Scotia coast and waited for McCoy's directions. McCoy didn't know what to do or where to send the boat. He knew his boat couldn't enter an American port with its illegal cargo. He also knew that it couldn't enter a Canadian port because its papers were out of order and he would thus have a hard time getting it out of port. While trying to decide what to do, McCoy went to Halifax, where he met a man who turned out to be a ship agent and merchant from St. Pierre and Miquelon. Before long, McCoy and the ship agent had struck a deal—McCoy would send his ship to St. Pierre for repairs and the man would act as his agent there.

When McCoy reached the island, he found a sleepy fishing community with tiny houses, a stone beach, and hills covered with drying codfish. There were no signs of the rum trade, but McCoy and his boat were warmly greeted.

News of the *Arethusa's* welcome reception on its first visit to St. Pierre travelled quickly via McCoy's customers in New York and other big cities along the American East Coast. Big players in the trade immediately saw a bonanza in St. Pierre. Even

St. Pierre

The St. Pierre waterfront in the 1930s

Why did St. Pierre become one of the chief liquor supply sources for the United States during Prohibition? After a short post-war period of trans-border smuggling between Canada and the U.S., the two countries' governments made agreements to shut down most of the liquor traffic between them. When that happened, distillers in Canada turned to offshore bases—like St. Pierre and Miquelon, a French territory—to legally export their products. Whiskies and other beverages were warehoused on these offshore bases until they were sold and loaded onto vessels cleared for improbable destinations. Instead of heading for the cleared destinations, the ships would then run the liquor off the American eastern seaboard, where they would anchor and await the small, fast launches that would shuttle the booze to shore.

Al Capone, whom McCoy may have worked for, is said to have spent time at the Hôtel Robert in St. Pierre.

More rum-running ships soon arrived in St. Pierre, creating a warehousing crisis on the island. When all of the normally available storage space was filled, rum-runners used basements and sheds to house their crates of alcohol. As the fishermen on the island began to abandon their trade to become stevedores, warehousemen, and cartage operators, there were fewer fish to process, and St. Pierre's largest building—a new fish processing plant—was converted into a giant liquor warehouse with a dock available at its door for freighters to tie up alongside.

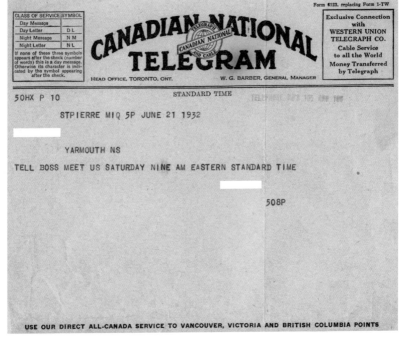

Telegrams sent from St. Pierre and Boston with instructions for rum-runners

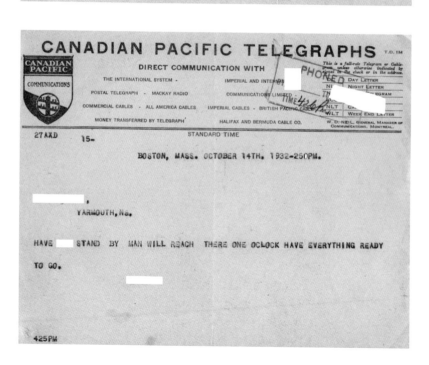

CLASS OF SERVICE	SYMBOL
Day Message	
Day Letter	D L
Night Message	N M
Night Letter	N L

If none of these three symbols appears after the check (number of words) this is a day message. Otherwise its character is indicated by the symbol appearing after the check.

CANADIAN NATIONAL TELEGRAM

HEAD OFFICE, TORONTO, ONT.   W. G. BARBER, GENERAL MANAGER

Form 6123, replacing Form 1-TW

Exclusive Connection
with
WESTERN UNION
TELEGRAPH CO.
Cable Service
to all the World
Money Transferred
by Telegraph

STANDARD TIME

58HX N 25 NL

FOR PROMPT SERVICE
Telephone No 105 or 106

STPIERRE MIQ JAN 19 1933

YARMOUTH NS

COULD YOU EITHER WRITE OR WIRE EXPLAINING TROUBLE
AND IF   ANY CONNECTION   WITH SAME STOP ALL KINDS
OF STORIES GOING ON HERE

1032P

CANADIAN PACIFIC TELEGRAPHS   T.D. 1M

DIRECT COMMUNICATION WITH

THE INTERNATIONAL SYSTEM -   IMPERIAL AND INTERNAT

POSTAL TELEGRAPH - MACKAY RADIO   COMMUNICATIONS LIMITED

COMMERCIAL CABLES - ALL AMERICA CABLES   IMPERIAL CABLES - BRITISH PACIFIC CABLE

MONEY TRANSFERRED BY TELEGRAPH   HALIFAX AND BERMUDA CABLE CO.

This is a full-rate Telegram or Cablegram unless otherwise indicated by signal in the clock or in the address.

DL   Day Letter
NL   Night Letter
NLT   ...
WLT   Week End Letter

W. D. NEIL, GENERAL MANAGER OF COMMUNICATIONS, MONTREAL.

27AXD   15-   STANDARD TIME

BOSTON, MASS. OCTOBER 14TH, 1932-250PM.

YARMOUTH, NS.

HAVE   STAND BY MAN WILL REACH THERE ONE OCLOCK HAVE EVERYTHING READY
TO GO.

425PM

In 1922, the once-quiet fishing community saw five hundred thousand cases of liquor pass through and more than one thousand vessels enter into its port. St. Pierre eventually surpassed the Bahamas in number of cases of liquor shipped to the United States.

Soon the liquor unloaded amounted to ten gallons a week for every man, woman, and child on the islands of St. Pierre and Miquelon. Some structures on the islands were even built out of discarded liquor cases, and the fog rolling up the streets from the docks was often said to carry the scent of Scotch.

Empty **wooden liquor crates** were a boon to residents of St. Pierre and Miquelon. There were few trees on the islands, and wood from the more than 350,000 wooden cases and barrels that arrived in a year created a building materials boom. Many of the homes built during that era were made out of wooden liquor crates.

Delighted by the unexpected windfall, St. Pierre promptly imposed a four-cent-per-bottle tax on imports, and used the revenues to dredge away sandbars across the inner harbour so that the large freighters from distilleries could unload straight onto the docks.

By the mid-1920s, all of the major Canadian distillers had opened agencies on St. Pierre. The Bronfman family, owners of the Seagram Company, were soon the French colony's largest traders, using both Atlas Shipping and a new corporate umbrella called the Northern Export Company. Much of the high-quality Canadian whisky and rum warehoused on St. Pierre came via the St. Lawrence Seaway from the Bronfmans' distillery in the Montreal suburb of LaSalle, Quebec.

"THEY WANTED HIM BAD"

By early 1923, Rum Row was in its heyday. Fortunes were being made and the exploits of "The Real McCoy" were becoming legend. On one trip, the *Arethusa* left Nassau with $171,000 worth of booze on board, which was sold on Rum Row for $342,000. Once it arrived on land, the liquor's value jumped to $684,000. By the time dealers onshore cut it—one part liquor to three parts water and grain alcohol—and sold it to their customers, the load fetched $2 million.

However, with cash and alcohol flowing, trouble between rum-runners and government began to brew. "By the government's own admission we were not breaking a law," McCoy later argued. McCoy felt he wasn't breaking any Prohibition laws because he wasn't bringing his liquor into American-controlled water, where buying and selling alcohol was illegal during Prohibition. "We lay the distance offshore that the State Department had stipulated. We sold our cargoes on what

"BILL" McCOY WAS HERE ON SATURDAY

Famous Skipper, Known as "King of Rum Row" Made Flying Visit to Halifax.

A headline from the July 17, 1923, edition of the *Halifax Chronicle* describing a visit Bill McCoy made to the Halifax Hotel

was then termed the high seas. Legally we felt that the [U.S. Coast Guard's] cutters' intrusions were unjust. It was their business, we held, to keep boats from coming and going between the Row and shore, not to sniff around pious rum-runners on their lawful occasions."

The authorities likely felt that McCoy's notoriety was making a mockery of their efforts to enforce the laws of Prohibition. Despite McCoy's self-declared piety, one Coast Guard officer said at the time, "They wanted him bad in Washington." Capturing McCoy would not only boost the Coast Guard's image, but also send a signal to other smugglers that it was getting serious. In 1923, the U.S. Department of Justice ordered the Coast Guard to seize McCoy's schooner if found within twelve miles of shore and to arrest McCoy.

McCoy knew the U.S. Coast Guard was watching him closely, so he renamed the *Arethusa* the *Tomoka* and placed the boat under British registry. This meant that he would be beyond U.S. jurisdiction as long as he remained on the high seas.

On November 24, 1923, the authorities caught up with McCoy off Seabright, New Jersey. Revenue agents boarded the *Tomoka* and ordered it to follow the Coast

BIG CARGO OF BOOZE

The British schooner Tomoka, which put into port Monday night enroute from Nassau to St. Pierre, anchoring in Dartmouth Cove, has 5,200 cases of whiskey in the hold and is being watched by the Customs. When she was entered yesterday at the custom house her entry stated that she put in for engine repairs and to land a sick man Captain Downey, her skipper, has been admitted to hospital since the vessels' arrival here.

An article in the January 17, 1923, edition of the *Halifax Chronicle* describing the *Tomoka*'s arrival in Halifax with a load of whisky

Guard cutter *Seneca* into port. McCoy tried to make a run for freedom while some of the agents were on board. But when *Seneca* fired on the *Tomoka*, McCoy finally surrendered. The seizure was upheld, and two years later *Tomoka* was auctioned off. That same year, McCoy was jailed for nine months for rum-running. He was released on Christmas Eve 1925.

In the mid-1930s, McCoy learned that the *Saucy Arethusa*, as *Tomoka* was then known, had been working in the fish trade since its sale, but had run aground off the Sambro Ledges in Nova Scotia. McCoy made a trip to Nova Scotia to see it for the last time and to gather some memorabilia. Mourning the *Tomoka's* demise, he cut the main beam, where its registry tonnage had been carved, from his beloved fishing schooner and took it home to remind him always of its glory days.

CHAPTER 3

HOW THE OPERATION RAN

W<small>ORKING</small> aboard the Liverpool, Nova Scotia-based *Harbour Trader*, Hugh Corkum had many of the same experiences as thousands of other Maritime rum-runners. After sailing to the islands of St. Pierre and Miquelon to load his boat with liquor, he would travel to Rum Row off the coast of New York to sell it off the side of his boat to Americans who couldn't buy liquor in the country during Prohibition. Corkum joined the *Harbour Trader* as a sailor in early 1928. Built in Shelburne, Nova Scotia, a couple of years earlier, the boat was along the lines of an American ocean tugboat, 140 feet in length, with a cargo capacity of 4,600 cases of liquor, and a mast that was hinged for going under bridges. According to Corkum, "She was the pride of the fleet: majestic, streamlined, and one of the most notorious rum-runners in what was known as the Banana Fleet, which operated out of Liverpool, Nova Scotia."

With all the comforts of home, the *Harbour Trader* and its crew of ten would generally spend two weeks per month delivering liquor. The crew consisted of a captain, a mate, two engineers, four sailors, a radio wireless operator, and a supercargo (a person employed on board a vessel by the cargo owner).

“ It was an exciting experience, steaming up the bay towards Coney Island. Traffic was always heavy, and there were lights along the shore. The farther one got into the bay, the more tense it became. I vividly remember the manoeuvring we had to do to get past a four-stacker which was patrolling back and forth by Sandy Hook or Highland Light on the Jersey side, close to the entrance of New York Harbour. A four-stacker was a four-funnelled destroyer

Hugh Corkum

used at that time as a patrol ship on the American coast. The cutter would continually patrol back and forth at a slow rate of speed, with her bright searchlight scanning the horizon and surrounding water. The beam of light would penetrate the darkness for a long distance. The trick was to get past the cutter on the eastern side while she was headed towards the Jersey side. It was a scary feeling when the four-stacker put the searchlight beam in our direction. Many times I was sure they saw us, but lo and behold the searchlight would sweep away in another direction. How we always managed to escape unnoticed is still a mystery to me. We had been told that once they issued a warning to stop, if the order was disobeyed or ignored, they would use their fire-power without hesitation. ”

—Hugh Corkum on his experiences working on a rum-running boat

The crew on the *Harbour Trader* made decent wages for the standards of the time. Sailors were paid $75 a month plus a $150 bonus for every load of cargo successfully landed, which was more than some college-graduate engineers were making at the time. The captain made $300 monthly plus a $750 bonus for every trip landed.

A typical trip for the *Harbour Trader* would begin with a 375-mile run from Liverpool to St. Pierre to pick up a cargo of assorted liquors bound for New York. Cargo consisted of everything from whisky to champagne. "We took on almost everything except rum. Evidently, during that time period rum was not a very saleable refreshment on the New York market, even though it was the favourite drink among our crew," Corkum wrote in his book, *On Both Sides of the Law*.

The supply ship *Flora Anne* with the unregistered speedboat *Hobo*

After spending a few days in St. Pierre loading liquor, the crew would leave for New York. The trip was dangerous, most often during the cold winter months. Corkum wrote,

> Sometimes, especially during the winter months, it would be a long, rough and tiring trip bucking the westerly gales until we arrived off the American coast. At times during the winter we would heave to and pound ice off the superstructure. It was a wet, cold, slippery, dangerous job which had to be done, otherwise the ship would become top-heavy, unmanageable, and hard to steer. We carried large wooden mallets for that special purpose.
>
> Generally we proceeded along the coast of Nova Scotia and made our departure from Brazet Rock for the American coast. We would stay a considerable distance offshore when approaching the American coast in order to keep away from the American [U.S. Coast Guard] cutters who rarely ventured more than one hundred miles offshore.

When approaching the American coast, the crew on the *Harbour Trader* would receive instructions via shortwave wireless radio to stand by for a run to a designated spot, known as a "drop." They would time their arrival to the drop for after dark to avoid being detected by authorities. Once they reached the drop, they would be met by a cluster of open-decked speedboats, which would shuttle the booze to shore.

A GOOD BOAT

Getting liquor to customers off Rum Row required a good boat. During the early years of Prohibition in the United States, liquor was delivered in a variety of ships. Rum-runners used both two- and three-masted vessels, as well as the occasional sailing

A rare photo of men transferring alcohol in kegs from a supply ship to a contact boat

vessel without an engine. But as the U.S. Coast Guard's surveillance became more sophisticated, these slower boats proved unsuitable for the trade. Faster boats were needed.

The construction of new boats designed specifically for the liquor trade fell largely to Nova Scotian boat builders. The first boats built specifically for rum-running were launched in 1926 and Nova Scotian shipbuilders continued constructing rum-running boats until 1933. The communities of Meteghan and Shelburne were the principal centres of Nova Scotia's rum-running boat trade. During the period from 1926 to 1933, twenty-five boats were built in Meteghan and twenty-two in Shelburne. To a lesser extent, boats were also built in Lunenburg, Mahone Bay, Liverpool, and Dayspring.

The six vessels built to carry liquor in Meteghan in 1928 were more than 87 feet each in registered length and more than 87 gross tons. By 1930, rum-running boat lengths had increased to well over 98 feet and gross tonnage to 118. The design of the boats had also undergone a significant change—the small, flush-decked, double-ended boats built originally as small diesel-powered coastal freighters had developed transom sterns, stouter construction, and a low trim profile. These new boats lay lower in the water, and were thus harder for authorities to detect.

The rum-runner *Selma K*, which was built in 1927 in Shelburne, Nova Scotia

The rum-runner *Lomergain*, which was built in 1929 by Ernst S. B. Co. Ltd. in Mahone Bay, Nova Scotia. In 1937, it was renamed *Martha Page*.

Rum-running boats were usually lean little craft designed to be ignored or overlooked. In general, rum-running boats were long, slim, low (especially when loaded), and wooden, with slight sheers toward their bows, and sometimes with raised forecastles. Their deck houses were low, single-deck structures, with slightly raised wheelhouses forward. Each boat usually had a small cargo hatch fore and aft, and a dory stowed on very light davits on the aft deck. To remain anonymous, most boats were painted grey. For safety, the wheelhouse windows were fitted with portable steel shutters that were secured over the glass when the boats reached Rum Row to protect the crew from gunfire from pirates or the U.S. Coast Guard. Rum-runners were easy to drive, but they were not fast boats—their cruising speeds were usually only ten to twelve knots. The faster boats were the forty-knot contact boats that carried the liquor from the rum-runners to the shore bases.

The *Placentia*, a rum-runner built in 1930 in Meteghan, Nova Scotia

The *Nan and Edna*, a rum-runner built in 1929 in Meteghan, Nova Scotia

The *Miserinko*, which was built specifically for rum-running

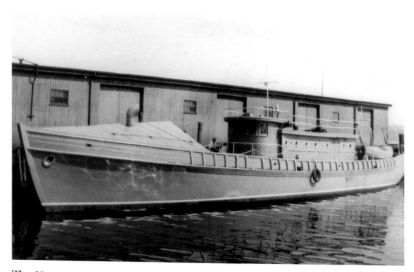

The *Yamasaka*, a rum-runner built by J. MacLean and Sons in Mahone Bay, Nova Scotia. It was renamed *Andrava* in 1934.

THE *REO II*

T HE *REO II* was one of the most famous Meteghan-built rum-
runners. Built in 1931 and designed specifically for the rum
trade, it had a low silhouette and was painted a drab grey colour,
making it hard for the U.S. Coast Guard to detect.

As a captain on the *REO II*, Aubrey Backman of Lunenburg
made countless trips to the United States with loads of liquor.
On a good trip, he could go from Nova Scotia to St. Pierre, then
to a drop point off the American coast, and back to Nova Scotia
in nine days.

On one moonless night during Prohibition, Captain Backman and the crew of the *REO II* waited silently just outside the
twelve-mile limit off a New Jersey beach. A smaller, faster vessel

The *REO II* in Meteghan, Nova Scotia, 1931

slipped through the dark waters and came to the *REO II*'s side. The crews of both vessels quickly started to move cases of whisky from the *REO II* to the speedboat. Only a dozen of the four hundred cases had been transferred to the smaller boat when a U.S. Coast Guard cutter, less than fifty yards away, snapped on a blinding searchlight. The Coast Guard had been tipped off to the position and time of the drop, and the *REO II* and speedboat found themselves trapped in the middle of a triangle formed by three Coast Guard cutters.

"I started the *REO [II]*'s engine and covered the speedboat from the cutter's light while the crew dumped the twelve cases," Captain Backman recalled. By the time one of the cutters reached the speedboat to search it, the cases had all been dumped. But as Captain Backman explained, "The Yanks had been a little too anxious. If they had waited until we had more

Cargo List for the *REO II*'s Second-Last Trip During Prohibition:

700 cases Dougherty pints
280 cases Lincoln Inn pints
250 cases Golden Wedding pints
100 cases Lincoln quarts
50 cases Ambassador quarts
40 cases Robbie Burns reputed quarts
25 cases Noilly pints
150 cases Four Aces pints
100 cases Weston Imperial quarts
75 cases Weston reputed quarts
200 cases Pikeville pints
225 cases Old Crow pints
675 cases Guggenheim pints
100 cases Jessie Moore pints
100 cases Peter Pan pints
50 cases Deluxe Bourbon pints
10 cases Deluxe Bourbon quarts
100 cases Stewart Rye pints
15 cases Blue Grass pints
15 cases Glenmore pints
25 cases Early Times quarts
10 cases Peter Pan quarts

of the whisky transferred, we couldn't have had time to dump it and they would have had us."

After the speedboat was taken in tow, Captain Backman headed toward the Nantucket lightship (a lightship is a ship that acts as a lighthouse) under the watchful eye of one of the cutters. "The lightship was always a good place to lose the Coast Guard," Captain Backman explained. "We'd make a few turns around the ship then head off on a straight course with our lights cut. We'd lose 'em that way." The *REO II* circled the lightship and then turned off all its lights to confuse the Coast Guard. Once it lost the Coast Guard boat that was following it, it continued on its course.

Captain Backman had many other close calls while running liquor on the *REO II*. "Sometimes it got pretty hot," he recalled. "During the winter of 1932 and 1933, we were chased off the American coast

THE END OF THE *REO II*

The *REO II* only spent five of its fifty-four years as a rum-runner. When Prohibition ended, the boat was used as a coastal freighter, and during World War Two it was taken over by the navy and used as a minesweeper in Shelburne, Nova Scotia.

In 1970, the boat was purchased by the Lunenburg Marine Museum Society and put on display at the Fisheries Museum of the Atlantic in Lunenburg. In 1984, a survey done by marine architects determined it was not practical to repair the boat, which was battered from over fifty years of wear and tear.

On February 24, 1985, the *REO II* was towed from its berth at the Fisheries Museum of the Atlantic and scuttled at an explosive dumping range roughly thirty-five miles northeast of Halifax.

The *REO II* outbound from Liverpool Bay, Nova Scotia, March 18, 1938

by the cutters several times. They would make sweeps around the *REO II* firing machine guns. There was one bullet hole in the main mast fourteen inches above the wheelhouse. That's getting a bit too close. I'll tell you, I was some happy when we came back to Nova Scotia for the last time."

EVADING AUTHORITIES: RADIO AND CODES

Radios were valuable tools for rum-runners. Some rum-runners only had radio receivers, which skippers used to receive the orders for drop-off locations. Other rum-runners had more sophisticated naval radio direction finders, which enabled them to call direction finder stations for bearings in order to locate Coast Guard surveillance boats. The rum ships equipped with a radio would request their bearings by international code. The stations would give them the information, usually without knowing the identity of the vessel. But before long, the stations caught on and started passing on the bearings of the rum ship to the Coast Guard cutter in the area.

After the rum-running business was taken over by large American organized crime syndicates, which had more money for accessories and equipment, most rum-running boats were equipped with radios. The rum-runners used the radios to receive clandestine messages in special codes. Since the codes were

RULES FOR RADIO OPERATORS

Below is an example of the instructions a radio operator on board a rum-running boat might receive.

• If no other appointment has been made upon leaving port, operator aboard ship will listen in at 10:00, 11:00, and 11:59 PM. Eastern Standard Time each night until communication is established with land station.

• Operator aboard ship will listen in the first ten minutes and if after the first ten minutes he does not hear the land station, he will then broadcast any message he may have been expecting the land station to pick up. When communication is established, land station will then give OK for the messages.

• Land station will always call first unless otherwise agreed.

• All messages will be in code.

• All appointments will be made by Eastern Standard Time.

(From the Baker collection at the Yarmouth County Museum and Archives)

RUM-RUNNING RADIO CODES

```
      MONDAY              BOAT # 3
BOAT-TO-SHORE = CRD
SHORE -TO- BOAT = M7
      TUESDAY
BOAT  TO  SHORE = DAS
SHORE  TO  BOAT = CM
      WEDNESDAY
BOAT  TO  SHORE = JOY
SHORE  TO  BOAT = OH
      THURSDAY
BOAT  TO  SHORE = LVI
SHORE  TO  BOAT = 6Y
      FRIDAY
BOAT  TO  SHORE = XYZ
SHORE  TO  BOAT = SU
      SATURDAY
BOAT  TO  SHORE = PIZ
SHORE  TO  BOAT = Q9
      SUNDAY
BOAT  TO  SHORE = DVD
SHORE  TO  BOAT = AF
```

A set of coded rum-running instructions

Examples of codes used by rum-runners:

MAL=North
MAM=South
MAO=East
MAP=West
MIR=Law has stopped us
MIS=Law is going to take us in
MIT=Law is firing on us
MFH=How many boats are you sending out?
MHA=What is your weather?
MEA=How far are you from ____?
MJR=We need assistance. Send out another boat to help.

just meaningless conglomerations of letters, usually in groups of ten, the messages meant nothing to others. But to those involved in rum-running, they contained essential information—daily liquor sales, daily receipts, the quantity of contraband remaining on board, and the exact location of a vessel. They also provided the ships with information regarding the locations of the rendezvous spots where they were to drop the liquor, the names of the contact boats, and the specific cargoes to be transferred.

To further avoid the authorities, the rum-runners' shore-based radio stations went underground and operated outside the law. These illegal stations used radio frequencies that would attract the least attention and cause the least interference, and moved frequently to evade prosecution by the Federal Communications Commission.

One of the tricks some rum-runners liked to play was to put in a distress call to the Coast Guard. Coast Guard cutters would be sent to the scene of "distress," but instead of finding an emergency situation they wouldn't find anything. While the Coast Guard was tied up with the phoney distress call, the rum-runners would run their cargo to shore, taking advantage of the security gap created by the hoax.

EVADING AUTHORITIES: SMOKESCREENS AND TRAPS

Smokescreens were another method rum-runners used to avoid authorities. When a rum-running boat was detected, its crew often laid down a smokescreen, either by using a commercial smoke generator or by using the simpler method of lighting rags and oil on fire and adding the smoke to the boat's main engine exhaust.

A smokescreen could also be set up by using a tank connected by piping to an electrically driven pump, which in turn was connected to the exhaust manifold of the boat's engine. The tank was filled with oil, and the suction cock was opened on the bottom to let the oil run to the manifold. This would cause a very hot, black smoke to come out of the exhaust. When the smoke reached the air, it would hang low and heavy, causing a screen that couldn't be penetrated by sight or searchlight.

Some rum-runners also "trapped" their boats to avoid having authorities find their illegal cargo. A "trapped" craft was a boat that was altered so that it could carry rum or other alcohol in concealment. One method of trapping was to build doubled bulkheads (the walls in a ship that run crosswise to its length), leaving a cargo space between the walls where cases of liquor could be loaded. However, doing this would mean the smuggler might only be able to bring a few hundred cases on a ship that had capacity for several thousand.

EVADING AUTHORITIES: LEGAL LOOPHOLES

A large part of rum-runners' operations involved avoiding the legal authorities, often in creative ways. For example, the *Fanny Powell* docked in St. Pierre and loaded a full shipment of whisky, which was to be delivered to Joseph's Inlet, near New York. The *Powell* then sailed to the rendezvous position on the instructions given to its captain via a coded message.

Just as the final load on board the *Fanny Powell* had been slung over the side onto a smaller contact vessel, a large U.S. Coast Guard cutter fired warning shots at the rum-runners. The authorities approached the *Powell* and questioned its captain. Asked for an explanation, the captain claimed that his ship was leaking and that he was merely transferring his cargo to another vessel in an effort to save the ship and its cargo. The Coast Guard allowed the Powell to proceed, but took the smaller vessel in tow and impounded both the ship and its cargo. The liquor was then transferred to a warehouse on the New York waterfront where seized cargoes were held.

The owner of the liquor knew he was in trouble, so he hired Louis Halle, a New York lawyer renowned for successfully defending rum-runners. Halle fought the case on the grounds that the *Powell* had been sinking, and the judge ruled that the cargo should be released. The *Powell*'s owner sailed into New York to pick up his liquor, but when he arrived at the warehouse he discovered that due to careless handling and stacking it was impossible to separate his goods from the other seized material. By greasing the hands of the warehouse men, he took back more liquor than had been seized from his vessel. Clearing New York in a hurry, he set off for the coast of Maine, where he sold the bottled goods without difficulty.

EVADING PIRATES

R**UM-RUNNERS** not only had to evade the U.S. Coast Guard and Royal Canadian Mounted Police, but also pirates, who soon became their worst foes. For example, on March 11, 1922, the Yarmouth, Nova Scotia, schooner *Eddie James* sailed into Halifax Harbour. Some days earlier, it had left Halifax for New Jersey with six hundred cases of liquor. It had anchored in the waters outside of New Jersey and had already sold some of its cargo when a launch from a large steamer had drawn alongside of it and five men had come over the side with pistols. The pirates fired shots, hitting and wounding the supercargo. Two of the

" It was scary out there. I don't know who we were more worried about: the Coast Guard cutters or the gangsters on Rum Row who wanted to hijack our load. "

—*Clem Hiltz, a former rum-runner*

pirates then held the crew at bay while the others removed the remaining cargo and eight hundred dollars in cash. The pirates escaped, taking the wounded man with them.

As pirates began attacking rum-runners, more and more liquor smugglers began dumping booze overboard or hiding it in the swamps and woods on islands throughout the Maritimes. It was not uncommon for residents to find liquor that had been hidden for later retrieval.

According to one tale, a young boy, who lived near Chester Basin, Nova Scotia, was walking along the beach one evening when he noticed a piece of paper between two rocks. He bent down to pick it up and found that it was attached to a long piece of string that was buried in a few inches of sand. He followed the string to an old maple tree, where it suddenly disappeared into the earth. He dug until a huge hole opened. In the hole he found a rum-runner's stash.

The string was looped through the handles of eight one-gallon ceramic jugs filled with Cuban cane rum. The boy covered up the hole with branches and ran to tell his grandfather. They came back and hauled out the jugs. They then tied the string to the horns of an old bleached cattle skull, which they placed in the hole. They refilled the hole and covered up the string along the beach. They laughed, thinking about how surprised the rum-runners would be when they returned for their stash. When they got back to the grandfather's farm they hid the jugs beneath the floorboards of the barn.

CHAPTER 4

DANGER ON THE SEAS: NOVA SCOTIA'S *I'M ALONE*

THE Lunenburg-based *I'm Alone* was probably the most notorious rum-running boat registered in Nova Scotia during Prohibition. Its incredible story became fodder for folklore and legend.

In the fall of 1928, a U.S. rum-running syndicate sent its agent, "Big Jamie" Clark, to Nova Scotia to find a vessel suitable for the trade. In Lunenburg, he found the *I'm Alone*, a 125-foot, 2-masted, 90-ton net schooner with a cargo-carrying capacity of 250 tons. Five years earlier, the *I'm Alone* had been launched in Lunenburg as hundreds of people

Captain John "Jack" Thomas Randell with his wife, Gertrude

crowded into the shipyard to watch. It was one of five ships built in the town in 1923 by the same shipyard that built the famous schooner *Bluenose*. A Boston gangster had commissioned the building of the *I'm Alone* in order to smuggle whisky from Canada to the United States. Equipped with a jib, jumbo, foresail, and storm trysail, the *I'm Alone* averaged a speed of about nine knots. Fortunately, the boat didn't have to rely solely on the wind; it also sported two Fairbanks-Morse semi-diesel, oil-burning, hundred-horsepower engines.

Clark liked the schooner and bought it for eighteen thousand dollars. He then began his search for a skipper. It wasn't long before he found Captain Jack Randell, a tough Newfoundland-born skipper and decorated war veteran. Randell's motto was said to have been, "Once a scrapper, always a scrapper."

Clark offered Randell a retainer (a preliminary payment to secure services) of five hundred dollars a month, plus a bonus at the end of the job, to take command of the *I'm Alone* and run booze along the Louisiana coast. Randell took some time to ponder the offer. "Rum-running was beginning to pall," Randell later explained. "I had undergone some unfortunate experiences in it. I had risked my own life. I had been cheated and swindled. I had been thrown in contact with some of the toughest and crookedest characters any man could meet. The adventure and the possible profits could not wholly outweigh what I had been through." Despite all this, Randell decided to accept the offer. He later said that he preferred "a winter in tropical waters at good pay, as against a winter in Nova Scotia in enforced idleness."

Randell's first trip on the *I'm Alone* was to St. Pierre to load up with liquor. The *I'm Alone* could carry about 2,800 cases. After paying eighty cents per quart for the booze, Randell and his crew sold it on Rum Row for forty dollars per twelve-quart case.

By the late 1920s, the methods rum-runners used for selling liquor had changed. The days had gone when it paid to drop anchor on Rum Row and peddle the liquor in small quantities to whomever had cash to pay for it over the side. The procedure had become more systematized, and the syndicate Randell worked for was a sophisticated one. Before the liquor was even loaded onto the schooner, the syndicate had a buyer lined up in the United States. Even the price was settled in advance.

Under this system, Randell was under strict orders to remain on the high seas, outside American territorial waters. He wouldn't even know the name of the man who came to get the liquor. But identifying him was simple.

CAPTAIN JACK RANDELL

Jack Randell was known as a daredevil on the sea. Having served with the Royal Navy in World War One, he won the Distinguished Service Cross and the Croix de Guerre for a skirmish with a German U-boat. Something of a character, when he went aboard the *I'm Alone*, his travelling gear included a suit of tails, six dress shirts, twelve dress collars, eighteen pairs of silk socks, and a collapsible opera hat.

Before Randell sailed, he was given a packet of American one-dollar bills torn in half, with one chosen for identification. For example, he might be given fifteen half-banknotes, their serial numbers running consecutively. The eighth of those fifteen banknotes might be the one selected for identification.

He would then take the *I'm Alone* to the designated anchorage spot off the American coast and outside American territorial water, where another boat would come alongside.

"Who are you?" Randell would ask.

If the other captain was the right man, he would reply with a serial number. If it was the number from the eighth bill in Captain Randell's stack, the other captain would be permitted to board. The two captains would then produce the two half-banknotes. If the torn edges fit, Randell would give the other captain the liquor.

On one trip in November 1928, Randell sailed the *I'm Alone* out of Halifax to St. Pierre and picked up 1,500 cases of liquor before heading south again. He was given sealed orders and told not to open them until he reached Havana, Cuba. When he opened them, they contained instructions to proceed to a spot off the Louisiana coast, where he was to meet another boat. But before he could do that, the U.S. Coast Guard cutter *Walcott* started trailing the *I'm Alone*.

That night, Randell and his crew managed to get out of the cutter's sight. With Randell running the schooner without lights, the ships passed at short range without the *I'm Alone* being detected. Randell had even insisted that crew go down below to the engine room to smoke for fear that the glow of a cigarette would be seen by the authorities.

The next night, Randell was back in position, about one hundred miles offshore, south of the general steamer lane used by ships running between the Florida and Texas coasts. Randell was ready to deliver the liquor, but his counterpart didn't show up.

The crew of the *I'm Alone* waited in position for forty-eight hours before deciding to go to Belize to get in touch with the ship's owners by cable. Five days later, they reached their destination.

There was still no one there to meet him. "Have not met vessel to take cargo. Please wire instructions," Randell wrote.

The next day, he got a cable instructing him to go to a position thirty-five miles south of Trinity Shoal Light Buoy in Louisiana. After looking at a chart, he learned it would place him about sixty miles offshore. He arrived there and a fast motor cruiser came out to meet the boat just after dark.

"*I'm Alone* ahoy," a man called to Randell.

"Who are you and what do you want?" Randell asked.

"My serial number is Y28242814D," he called back.

Randell looked at the serial number of the first of the fifteen halves of torn American dollar bills that an agent in St. Pierre had given him. That was the number.

"Come alongside," he called to the man, who minutes later stepped aboard the I'm Alone.

"Show me your dollar bill," Randell demanded. The man handed it over. The ragged edges of the two half-banknotes matched exactly.

"How much can you carry?" he asked the man.

"About 1,200 cases," the man replied.

> " Those men are liars who tell you the days of adventure are dead. What they really mean is that they are dead, though the undertaker hasn't found it out yet. Adventure is a living thing, so long as there are men and women, sea and land, and ships to sail that sea on this planet. "

—*Captain Jack Randell*

On March 20, 1929, the *I'm Alone* dropped anchor for minor engine repairs, after sighting Trinity Shoal Light Buoy. Randell estimated they were about fourteen or fifteen miles off the U.S. coast. They had just over $62,000 worth of Scotch, rye, rum, and assorted champagnes and liqueurs on board. Around dawn, Randell spotted the U.S. Coast Guard cutter *Walcott* closing in fast from the west. Randell raised anchor and headed out to sea. By 6:30 AM, Captain Paul of the *Walcott* was close enough to shout, "Heave to!"

"I will not heave to!" Randell megaphoned back at him. "I'm on the high seas and you have no jurisdiction over me."

"I'll have to open fire on you if you don't heave to," Paul said.

"Shoot if you want," Randell replied.

Instead, Paul asked Randell if he could come aboard to talk. He rowed across in his dory still wearing his slippers. The two men talked about the situation.

Their dispute revolved around the *I'm Alone*'s position when first sighted by the Coast Guard. Under a doctrine called "hot pursuit," Paul was allowed to stop and search a suspected rum-runner if it was sighted less than twelve miles from shore. Paul argued that the *I'm Alone* was inside the treaty limits. After talking aboard the *I'm Alone* for close to two hours, he shook hands with Randell and went back to the *Walcott*.

The two boats continued on a southerly course out into the Gulf of Mexico. At about 2:00 PM, the *Walcott* raced up again. "Stop or I'll fire at you," Paul shouted. "I have orders to take you in. I will give you fifteen minutes to make up your mind. If you do not stop, I will be obliged to fire at you."

"I have no intention of stopping. You need not waste the fifteen minutes," Randell megaphoned back.

They continued sailing, and after about twenty minutes the first shot from the *Walcott* was heard. Paul fired a blank and then another. About twenty shots went through the *I'm Alone*'s sails.

"Suddenly I felt a sharp blow in the front of my right thigh. The whole leg went numb. I staggered but caught my balance. I looked down expecting to see the blood running," Randell later wrote.

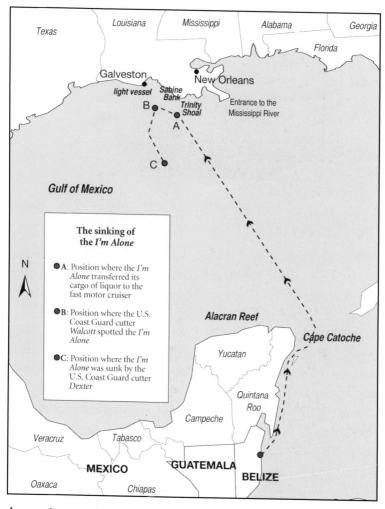

A map showing the location where the *I'm Alone* sank

SCHOONER SUNK; 2 DEAD

U. S. Coast Guard Sinks Fine Lunenburg - Built Schooner

SCHOONER IMALONE

A headline from the Saturday, March 23, 1929, edition of the *Halifax Chronicle* reporting on the sinking of the *I'm Alone*

Luckily for him, it was only a wax bullet. The *Walcott* soon ceased firing but continued to follow the schooner. For the next two days, Randell continued on his course, steering for a point about twenty miles east of the Alacran Reef off the coast of Mexico.

By daybreak on March 22, the wind had increased to a moderate gale. With its gun jammed and unable to fire, the *Walcott* radioed for help. The U.S. Coast Guard sent another boat, the *Dexter*. Its captain steered it alongside the *I'm Alone*.

Like Captain Paul had before him, Captain Powell of the *Dexter* shouted, "Heave to or I fire at you!"

Again Randell replied, "You have no jurisdiction over me and I refuse to stop."

The *Dexter* started firing four-pounder explosive shells, machine-gun bullets, and rifle bullets at the *I'm Alone*. "Shell

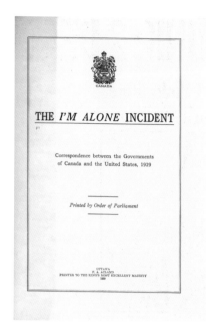

The official correspondence between Canada and United States about the *I'm Alone* incident

after shell ripped and tore through the upper works of the *I'm Alone*, smashing our booms, our boats, and our bulwarks," Randell recalled.

About thirty shells had hit the boat, none of them at the waterline or below it, when an order was shouted and firing ceased. "Now will you stop?" Powell asked.

"No, damn you! You may sink me if you like, but I will not surrender!" Randell shouted back.

The *Dexter* began firing at the water line. Shells tore into the hull of the *I'm Alone*. Water poured in. The crew began to jump overboard. The schooner went down, and with it went 2,800 cases of rum, brandy, and whisky.

"There I stood on the aft-deck, the last human being on the *I'm Alone*. Her forward deck was under water now. Then she began her last dive," Randell later wrote.

Randell was fished from the water by the Coast Guard and taken onto the *Dexter*. Powell ordered leg irons to be put around Randell's ankles. Twenty-four hours after Randell was rescued from the water, the *Dexter* and the *Walcott* moored at the U.S. Army engineers' wharf on the Mississippi River. Randell was taken to see the U.S. Coast Guard's base commander for the Gulf of Mexico.

"Gentlemen," he told a group of officials. "I wish to inform you that the sinking of my ship was a cowardly act, and that my crew and I were taken half-drowned out of the water more than one hundred miles from the coast of the United States of America. Under those circumstances I claim that you have no jurisdiction over me or my men. We are shipwrecked mariners. As such I demand that I be allowed to get in touch with my counsel and my owners immediately."

Randell was arrested and charged with conspiring to violate the laws of the United States. He and his entire crew—except Leon Maingoy, the boatswain, who had died as the *I'm Alone* sank—were sent to jail in New Orleans.

With Randell and his crew out on bail, the Canadian government pressed their case. The Canadians strongly protested the sinking as a breach of international law. The *I'm Alone*, they argued, had been outside American waters and beyond American laws at the time it was attacked.

Hardly a day went by between March 1928 and April 1929 that North American newspapers didn't carry the story. In Canada, the press hailed Randell as an international hero for upholding British naval traditions on the high seas. In Ottawa, one Member of Parliament called the sinking of the *I'm Alone* "an act of deliberate piracy" at best, and "an act of war" at worst.

The matter eventually went before an arbitration board, which decided that the U.S. Coast Guard had clearly violated international law by sinking the *I'm Alone*. In June 1929, in a written statement to the U.S. government, Canadian ambassador Vincent Massey filed a lawsuit demanding compensation for the crewmembers of the *I'm Alone* and their families, as well as a formal apology to Canada.

The United States eventually issued a formal apology and, in 1935, paid $25,000 to Canada as a show of regret for the insult to the Canadian flag, as well as $26,666.50 to the crew.

Randell received $7,906 of that money. He returned to Halifax and continued to earn his living as a sea captain on several ships. He enjoyed brief notoriety, and in 1930 he published *I'm Alone*, an autobiography detailing the experience. Randell died in his home in 1964 and was given a military funeral.

CHAPTER 5

NEW BRUNSWICK RUM-RUNNING, LAND AND SEA

NEW BRUNSWICK wasn't a particularly safe place in the late 1920s. As more and more liquor made its way through the province and smugglers grew more organized, the stakes became higher and violence more commonplace, with shootouts

The Violette Hotel in Saint-Léonard, New Brunswick, circa 1915

between gangsters and police or other law enforcement officials becoming common.

Albénie J. Violette (a.k.a. Joe Walnut) was the biggest and most ruthless of all the booze czars in New Brunswick. Operating out of his headquarters at the Brunswick Hotel in Saint-Léonard, Violette owned the largest and most modern illegal distillery in the province. He also controlled bottling plants and chartered ships that bought illicit alcohol from Europe and the West Indies.

Whiskey Sixes

Bootleggers travelling by car preferred large, specially outfitted, touring cars such as Studebakers, Hudsons, Chryslers, and other large sedans. They would remove the rear seats to make more room to carry liquor, and "soup up" the motors. Sometimes called "whisky sixes" because of their powerful six-cylinder engines, the rum-runners' vehicles were often equipped with spotlights to blind the eyes of pursuers by night and thirty-foot chains to raise huge clouds of dust along dirt roads.

Violette was based out of Madawaska County, in the northwestern part of the province. From there, a quick truck drive across the United States border could result in a hefty profit. Violette's Madawaska mob also had strong connections with other liquor hotbeds in New Brunswick, especially Kent County, where bringing in smuggled liquor from St. Pierre was one of the largest industries in the late 1920s.

On one occasion, Violette planned to personally run a shipment of liquor across the border. He deliberately let it be known to U.S. customs officials where and when he intended to hit the border. The American officers took precautions. Knowing the road he would be using, they built a barricade of logs and sawhorses and took up their positions awaiting his arrival.

Almost to the minute of the time Violette said he would arrive, he drove up to the border at more than fifty miles per hour. The waiting officials had formed a line across the road, and as the car approached they waved their arms and flashlights for him to stop. Violette ignored their cries. He held his foot on the accelerator and the men had no choice but to run. He kept going until he was a few yards from the barricade, then he put his foot on the brakes, cut to the side, and crashed through the barricade and into the ditch. Expecting to find him dead, the officers instead found a wrecked car and a raving man, who called them a bunch of "murderous and brainless idiots."

Violette had no booze in his car. While he continued his tirade against the officers, a truck approached the border from the Canadian side and sped on through into Maine with a load of contraband booze. The officers knew they had been duped and that Violette would be able to sue for the cost of his wrecked car and for endangering his life. That's exactly what he did. He eventually won a substantial settlement in a lawsuit.

With Prohibition still in effect in New Brunswick until the late 1920s, liquor was smuggled not only out of the province, but into it as well. In early September 1927, for example, rumours of a large quantity of booze coming from the United States and destined for Bathurst reached an excise officer named Arthur J. Meahan, who established a stakeout to apprehend the smugglers.

On the night of September 22, two suspicious cars with Maine licence plates were spotted heading toward Bathurst on the Bathurst-to-Miramichi highway (which was commonly referred to as "Benzine Boulevard" in the press because of the large amounts of alcohol transported across it). Immediately, Meahan and his partner engaged in hot pursuit. In a frantic effort to throw off the officers, the driver of the lead rum-running vehicle took his car off the highway, rolling it over in a ditch. The occu-

Bathurst, New Brunswick, circa early 1900s

pants escaped the vehicle and made off into a wooded area. The second car, which was also loaded with alcohol, headed toward South Bathurst. In an attempt to lose the law enforcers, the driver turned into a blind road. But when he found himself cornered, he fled the scene on foot. Meahan and his partner were not able to catch the rum-runners, but they did seize five hundred gallons of illegal alcohol from the cars.

As the decade wore on, New Brunswickers felt more and more like they were living in Al Capone's lawless Chicago. On June 25, 1930, Moncton residents woke to read the following headline in the *Moncton Times*: "Gun Battle Between Provincial Police and Rum Runners." The article went on to report a daring encounter:

> A car containing twenty gallons of alcohol was seized by Sergeant Carleton and Officer Teed after some fourteen shots had been exchanged. Occupants of the car escaped in darkness

near Cocagne. Illicit runners opened fire on the police when commanded to stop and police returned fire and pursued the rum-runners until the car was captured.... Three shots were fired at the police before the officers had a chance to return the fire and during the chase that followed some fourteen shots in all were fired by the police and pursued occupants of the liquor car. When the police gained on the vehicle, the occupants abandoned it, and the car continued on an erratic course. No arrests were made, the darkness favouring the illicit liquor conveyers, all of whom made good their escape.

RUNNING ON WATER

SITUATED on the coast of the Northumberland Strait, the Bouctouche-Richibucto region in the eastern part of New Brunswick was a principal centre of liquor smuggling. Rum-runners like Tom Nowlan and Oswald MacFadden would frequently travel to St. Pierre, load up their vessels with liquor, and return to satisfy New Brunswickers.

In New Brunswick, pure white alcohol was the preferred contraband. The favourite was Hand Brand, which was ninety-five percent pure alcohol. It was sold packed in cases that consisted of two three-gallon metal containers. Another popular variety of similar-strength alcohol was Star Brand, which was produced in Belgium. Both types were supplied in large quantities from St. Pierre.

New Brunswick customers also relied on Henri Moraze, a prominent liquor merchant in St. Pierre, for their liquor supply. Moraze would send his vessels to deliver alcohol to independent bootleggers in the province. The local dealers would visit Moraze's boats outside the territorial limit to load up their own boats with booze. Competition between the dealers was keen, with prices fluctuating depending on supply and demand.

It was often easier for Moraze to sell all of the alcohol on his boat to one person rather than deal with several buyers. On one occasion, Moraze wrote Nowlan from his schooner, "I am off the PEI coast and expect to be home in 10–15 days. I wanted to ask you if you could handle 500 barrels of 12 gallons of Belgian alcohol at $1.50 a gallon, delivered on your coast. The price is subject to a quick dispatch. […] The other day I was off Richibucto. They all wanted alcohol and I had at the time very little to offer so they asked me to come back with a load. I would rather do business with you and not bother with the others."

Moraze's desk was flooded with requests from independent liquor dealers in New Brunswick. Typical messages read, "I would like to buy $1,000 worth of alcohol as well as 25–30 cases of Scotch. Please come with your boat off the Bouctouche lighthouse, or if this is not convenient, come close to Bouctouche and Richibucto. Tell us as closely as possible what your position will be. Once you are there we will flash a light at you and you will answer us."

Although the liquor business was concentrated in the Bouctouche-Richibucto region, transactions also took place to a lesser degree along other portions of the New Brunswick coast facing the Northumberland Strait. Further north, huge liquor shipments were landed by schooner at Miscou Island in the Gulf of St. Lawrence and along the Caraquet coast.

CLAMP DOWN

By 1934, most New Brunswick bootleggers and rum-runners were feeling the noose tightening around them. In October of that year, the RCMP seized 1,580 gallons of alcohol stored in a barn in Belledune. Sergeant Bedford Peters assessed the haul at more than $55,000. Duty alone on the contraband was valued at $17,380. That same month, authorities seized the rum-running vessel *Paul T* in Shippagan. After confiscating the 1,200 gallons of alcohol and a large quantity of cigarettes on board the vessel and arresting the captain and crew, the law officials broke the boat up using saws and axes, destroyed the gasoline engine with sledgehammers, and burned the sails and rigging to set an example for other rum-runners.

By the end of the 1930s, the risky trade had come to a close. Prohibition had ended in New Brunswick in 1927 and even though the rum-runners could still turn a profit by undercutting the government liquor stores that were set up, the RCMP's enforcement work soon made rum-running too dangerous and unprofitable.

CHAPTER 6

LAST OF THE MARITIME RUM-RUNNERS: PRINCE EDWARD ISLAND'S *NELLIE J. BANKS*

PRINCE EDWARD ISLAND was the first province in Canada to get tough on alcohol. Prohibition hit the island in 1901, making it illegal to manufacture, sell, or possess alcohol. The exception to the rule was that doctors were allowed to prescribe small amounts of alcohol for patients who they felt needed it. However, these restrictions didn't put a dent in demand for alcohol—they simply made it more difficult to get a drink.

Without a reliable, legal supply, many people in the province turned to smugglers. The most famous of these smugglers were the Dicks brothers, Edward and John, from Georgetown. The Dicks brothers captained the *Nellie J. Banks*, the notorious rum-running schooner that was the main carrier of alcohol to and from Prince Edward Island between 1926 and 1938, according to Geoff and Dorothy Robinson's book, *The Nellie J. Banks*.

The *Nellie J. Banks* was built by Howard Allen of Allendale, Shelburne County, Nova Scotia, who had established a reputation as one of the finest small-vessel builders in the province. After several months under construction, the *Nellie J. Banks* was launched in late October 1910. With a black hull and bright orange dories, the seventy-foot vessel had a striking appearance. The press praised it at the time, saying, "Neatly rigged and carrying two topmasts, she looked more like a yacht than a fishing schooner, having a graceful sheer. Some declare that she is the nicest looking vessel that ever sailed out of Lockeport Harbour."

Before it became a rum-runner, the *Nellie J. Banks* was a fishing boat. In 1914, two years before being fitted with an engine, it sailed up the coast to catch bait herring near the Magdalen Islands. Over the next decade, the *Nellie J. Banks* fished mostly out of Lockeport, Nova Scotia. Some years the crew went off northern New Brunswick and Quebec to net mackerel, and in others to Portland, Maine, to catch swordfish. But with fish prices falling drastically in the first half of the 1920s, the owners and crews of fishing vessels like the *Nellie J. Banks* were left scrambling to make ends meet.

Around this time, two men from Charlottetown—Ray Clark and Captain Edward Dicks—were making plans to purchase a schooner to smuggle liquor to Prince Edward Island. They thought the *Nellie J. Banks* was perfect. They bought the boat in September 1926 for a sum believed to be two thousand dollars.

The two men were not strangers to the rum-running trade. Dicks had been involved in smuggling rum to Cape Breton in 1910, and Clark had an interest in the *Grace Hilda*, a boat that had brought liquor to Prince Edward Island in the early 1920s.

Dicks and Clark put the *Nellie J. Banks* to work delivering illegal alcohol. After bringing one load of liquor to Prince Edward Island in 1926, the *Nellie J. Banks* was wintered in Georgetown. During that time, Dicks was contacted by two Americans who wanted him to deliver a cargo of whisky. Dicks accepted the contract, but careless talk in Boston ended those plans; on June 2, 1927, the office of the Special Agency Service in Boston received word that one thousand cases of whisky were being shipped from Prince Edward Island concealed in

Foiling the Plan

A copy of the following letter was sent to the American Consul in Charlottetown to warn U.S. officials of Edward Dicks's plans for exporting a cargo of whisky to the U.S.:

Office of the Special Agents
1306-23-0
Treasury Department
United States Customs Service
Boston, Mass.
27 May, 1927
The Collector of Customs, Portland, Maine.

Sir:
This office has received information from a reliable source that within the next few days, there are to be shipped from Prince Edward Island several car loads of potatoes and that in these cars are to be concealed one thousand cases of whiskey which it is claimed is to arrive in PEI by boat.

The informant understands that the whisky will be concealed inside the potato sacks, although it may be possible they may be shipped in bulk and the cases of whisky concealed underneath. The cars in question are to be shipped from points on the Souris branch of the CNR operating on PEI and a party by the name of Brown in Rhode Island, possibly Woonsocket, is now negotiating the deal on the island.

It is understood that Vanceboro is to be the port of entry and therefore a copy is being sent to the Deputy Collector of Customs at the port for immediate action, although it may be advisable for you to advise all railway ports in your district of this information.

Respectfully,
Wm. B. Harney, Special Agent

carloads of potatoes. The authorities seized the liquor, but the Americans were the losers in the deal, as Captain Dicks had already been paid his freight.

GOOD FORTUNE ENDS

THE *Nellie J. Banks* outsmarted the authorities on numerous occasions, but the vessel's good fortune couldn't last forever, and it didn't. In July 1927, word spread quickly through Charlottetown

DICKS WILL LAY CHARGE OF PIRACY

Owner of the Schooner Nellie J. Banks, Seized by the Govt. Cutter Bayfield, to Proceed Against Bayfield Captain.

A headline from a July 1927 edition of the *Charlottetown Guardian* reporting on the seizure of the *Nellie J. Banks*

that a rum-laden vessel belonging to Captain Dicks had been seized in the Northumberland Strait by the RCMP cutter *Bayfield*. Newspapers reported that the *Bayfield* had nabbed the *Nellie J. Banks* off East Point and was towing it westward toward Charlottetown.

During the previous winter, Dicks had made arrangements to buy a large quantity of rum from the *Vivian Ruth*, a bigger schooner anchored nearby off Cape Breton. The rum was the best there was. Costing fifteen dollars in South America for a ten-gallon keg, over the side of a boat off Prince Edward Island, the rum could fetch forty dollars a keg. After receiving the rum from the *Vivian Ruth* shortly before the seizure, the *Nellie J. Banks* safely landed some liquor near East Point, Prince Edward Island. Captain Dicks held the remainder of the liquor on the *Nellie J. Banks* near the eastern end of the Northumberland Strait in what he believed to be international waters. A few days later, before he had an opportunity to unload the last shipment, the RCMP cutter *Bayfield* made its seizure. The *Nellie J. Banks* had 330 ten-gallon kegs of rum on board at the time.

The law stated that the skipper and crew of a vessel seized with liquor inside territorial waters could be charged under the Customs Act. However, the fate of a ship and its cargo ultimately rested with the minister in charge of the Customs Act, who would rule on what penalty to impose. Rum-runners knew that a combination of good legal advice and political pressure usually resulted in light punishment.

Captain Dicks was charged with attempting to defraud the revenue of Canada by avoiding payment of duty on the rum. His

BIG LIQUOR SEIZURE OFF PRINCE EDWARD ISLAND COAST

Revenue Cruiser Bayfield seizes eight hundred cases of mixed liquor from schooner, eighteen miles east of East Pont.

A headline from a July 1927 edition of the *Charlottetown Guardian* reporting on the seizure of the *Nellie J. Banks*

response to the seizure of the *Nellie J. Banks* was to wage a fierce public relations campaign, telling the press:

> I am not a law breaker. I am a legitimate business man, not a smuggler as is my reputation. Had I been caught inside the three-mile limit, the revenue cutter would have seized my schooner, taken the cargo, and had the crew arrested as soon as they reached port. It is the custom of the cutters outside the three-mile limit to confiscate the cargo and tell the schooner to get out of sight. My schooner had to be towed into port because it was taking water and the pumps had to be used to keep her floating. The crew wouldn't allow the cutter to remove the liquor. They were ordered to transfer the cargo, but refused to do so—the four men on board held out in the knowledge that the government officers would be loathe to use force outside the three-mile limit.
>
> In this case, they have seized the cargo of a schooner outside the three-mile limit. That's where I have them—they are pirates!

In the end, the authorities relented and had to admit that Dicks had not broken the law. The Crown was ordered to pay for the painting and repair of the schooner, which, according to Dicks, had been damaged when the government cutter rammed it. In addition, Dicks received $5,500 in damages and $700 for costs. It took nine months for Dicks to reach this settlement. Once the *Nellie J. Banks* was released, it was back in business.

For the next nine years, the *Nellie J. Banks* was a familiar sight off Prince Edward Island's shores from late May to late November. Though a small amount of the *Nellie J. Banks's* cargo was landed in Cape Breton and on the Magdalen Islands, the majority was picked up just beyond the three-mile limit, on the island's equivalent to Rum Row. Captain Dicks had lost interest in the vessel over the years and was no longer involved, but Ray Clark retained his ownership.

In 1938, the *Nellie J. Banks*'s rum-running days came to an end when the RCMP caught up with it for the last time. The ship was in the waters off Prince Edward Island one day in August when the RCMP cutter *Ulna* fired a blank shot at it and demanded that it stop. The RCMP officers boarded the vessel to check its papers and cargo. They were sure they would find illegal liquor on board. When asked about the cargo, the captain of the *Nellie* said, "I have a cargo of liquor but am well outside the three-mile limit."

The RCMP officer told the captain that a twelve-mile limit was in effect and that he was under arrest for having contraband goods in his possession, in contravention of the Customs Act. The case went to court, but the jury couldn't come to a unanimous decision. The Crown eventually dropped the case, believing that jurors in the province were sympathetic to rum-runners and would never convict them.

Shortly thereafter, the Department of Customs and Excise put what had then become the last of the Atlantic Canadian rum-runners up for sale. The *Nellie J. Banks* was bought by Captain John Maguire, master of the Prince Edward Island car ferry *Abegweit*. He renamed it the *Leona G. Maguire* after his daughter. After years of being improperly maintained, the boat became so run down that it was too expensive to repair. In 1953, it was torched and destroyed in Murray Harbour.

CHAPTER 7

EFFORTS TO QUASH RUM-RUNNING

Law enforcement officials on the East Coast had a tough job during Prohibition. The U.S. Coast Guard, the Canadian Preventive Service of the Customs Department, and the RCMP tried hard to enforce Prohibition, but they had to battle the many forces working against them. Not only did they have thousands of miles of Atlantic coastline and inland waterways to patrol, but also the New Brunswick border with the United States. They also faced a public that generally wanted its liquor and took a dim view of the work of law enforcement agencies.

DRY NAVY CLAIMS VICTORY

New York. Success continues to follow the "Dry Navy's" blockade of Rum Row, under the most difficult conditions. Today, the seventh of the blockade, was one of dense, swirling fog. It was just this kind of weather the "Dry Navy" commanders feared most as it would permit the rum-runners their best opportunity of running the blockade. But the government men averred that victory was with them—that, so far as they knew, not a bit of liquor had trickled into the country from Rum Row.

From the *Halifax Morning Chronicle*,
May 12, 1925

THE DANGERS OF RUM-RUNNING

On January 24, 1931, the Nova Scotia rum-runner *Josephine K* was captured by the U.S. Coast Guard cutter 145 at the entrance to New York Harbour. The captain of the *Josephine K*, William Pike Cluett of Lunenburg, was shot during the capture and died shortly thereafter. No other crewmembers were injured.

In 1927, the U.S. Coast Guard estimated that 158 rum-running boats were working the American coast. There was also an inshore fleet of several hundred faster motorboats and smaller vessels that were used to deliver booze to the shore.

Law officials were busy during what became known as "the lawless decade." In the period from the early 1920s until the early 1930s, federal Prohibition agents from the U.S. arrested 577,000 suspected offenders, and seized more than a billion gallons of illegal booze, 45,000 automobiles, and 1,300 boats believed to have played a part in the illicit trade. Yet despite all these arrests and seizures, it didn't make much difference. Lincoln C. Andrews, assistant secretary of the U.S. Treasury in charge of Prohibition enforcement, estimated in 1926 that less than five percent of the liquor smuggled into the United States was being seized.

Not only did the authorities' work not seem to make much of a dent in the smuggling, but worst of all, thousands of people

I was a teetotaller until Prohibition.

—American comedian Groucho Marx, capturing the mood of the times

The U.S. Coast Guard CG-100, one of the 203 seventy-five-foot patrol boats built specifically for Prohibition-enforcement duties.

were dying or being killed because of alcohol. Between 1920 and 1930, two thousand gangsters and five hundred Prohibition agents were reported killed in gunfights triggered by the trade.

UNINTENDED CONSEQUENCES

Liquor started pouring into the United States shortly after Prohibition came into effect. By failing to adequately enforce Prohibition in the United States, American law officials allowed Canada to become the principal supply source for drinkers south of the border. In 1924, Canadian exports of alcoholic beverages skyrocketed to $10 million from $3.1 million two years earlier.

The earliest U.S. Coast Guard reference to the growing alcohol trade was in its annual report for 1921. The Florida coast patrol was reported to be "particularly vigilant" in enforcing Prohibition, making "hundreds of trips" in support of federal Prohibition authorities and seizing several vessels.

It didn't take long for the Coast Guard to realize that its resources were completely inadequate to control the rising tide of seaborne liquor. Commandant William E. Reynolds of the Coast Guard reported in October 1923 that the present force was able to prevent "only a small part" of the illegal traffic, a traffic that he said was "entirely unprecedented in the history of the country."

KITTING UP

COMMANDANT Reynolds called for 20 additional cruising cutters, 203 cabin cruiser-type motorboats, 91 small speedboats,

The U.S. Coast Guard destroyer *Tucker*

A line of U.S. Coast Guard patrol boats

about 3,500 additional personnel, and more than $19 million in funding for the Coast Guard. The U.S. government gave the green light to the Coast Guard's use of 20 World War One destroyers, along with 203 cabin cruisers, 100 smaller boats, and the requested additional personnel. This was the Coast Guard's largest single increase in size in its history.

The most famous Coast Guard vessels that Reynolds added became known as "six-bitters." These stripped down, spiffed up, 75-foot patrol boats were built not for comfort, but for speed. Fast and tough, the powerful six-bitters could zip in and out of harbours at speeds of up to 30 knots, making them one of the Coast Guard's most valuable assets in the rum war.

When the Coast Guard's arsenal was at its peak, it had approximately 330 vessels of 75 feet or more in length. Likely about 200 vessels were at sea battling the "rummies" at any given time. But if those 200 vessels could have spread a cordon along the coasts, that would have meant about 1 vessel in the line every 25 miles, leaving a lot of room for the rum-runners to operate.

MR. X

The U.S. Coast Guard relied on informers to help them do their work. One such informer went by the alias "Mr. X." No one knew who he was, how he got his information, or where he operated from, but his information never failed. He spoke frequently on the phone to Captain E. D. Jones in New York, giving him names and descriptions of rum boats and telling him where they would be at certain times. The information Mr. X supplied to the Coast Guard led them to make several rum-boat seizures.

The larger Coast Guard cutters and destroyers were used for offshore work where the rum-runners' mother ships, which carried big quantities of liquor, stayed. The Coast Guard's inshore patrol boats screened the coast for the contact boats that made their runs to shore.

By 1924, Congress gave the Coast Guard approval to buy airplanes to add to its fleet. The Coast Guard purchased five biplanes. With his new fighting force, Reynolds felt he was well prepared for the battle that lay ahead.

In May 1925, the Coast Guard began what became

A gun crew on a U.S. Coast Guard destroyer prepares to fire one of the ship's batteries

known as the "Great Offensive," to drive the rum fleet off the northeast seaboard of the United States. The operation involved concentrating forces off New York and Block Island, which was located just over twelve miles south of the coast of Rhode Island, where the largest Rum Row existed. The U.S. Coast Guard called up every available vessel to catch and arrest rum-runners. The offensive continued until August 1925, but was beginning to slow as the Coast Guard cutters started wearing down and needing repairs. The Coast Guard made many seizures and deemed the operation a success, but in the process they stretched the service's resources to the limit.

CHANGE IN THE TERRITORIAL LIMIT

In 1924, a new international agreement between the United States and other

AVOIDING ARREST

One cold January night during Prohibition, the *Harriet Lane*, a 125-foot U.S. Coast Guard cutter, was patrolling off Gloucester, Massachusetts, when it spotted a suspected rum-runner. After the cutter put a spotlight on the rum-runner, it proceeded to pick up speed. The *Harriet Lane* gave whistle signals for the Halifax-based rum-runner, the *Firelight*, to heave to.

The vessel forged ahead and a chase ensued. Finally the *Harriet Lane* sent a boarding party over to the *Firelight*, where they found contraband. The Coast Guard seized the vessel within the twelve-mile limit, determining that the point of seizure was 7.8 miles from the Londoner beacon. The court upheld the seizure, but the *Firelight* was back rum-running before long. The Coast Guard eventually caught up with the boat again. Rather than submitting to arrest, the *Firelight* struck the pursuing Coast Guard patrol boat and sank.

important maritime nations increased the three-mile limit of national jurisdiction to a twelve-mile limit. The new agreement meant that the nations would recognize seizures of ships made not just three miles out—as they had in the early 1920s—but now twelve miles out.

The longer distances that the rum-runners were now forced to traverse to reach the supply ships in international waters caused the smugglers to develop a new tactic for transferring liquor. Instead of waiting in international waters for the contact boat to arrive, bigger rum ships would wait until dark, then run in as far as they dared to pre-arranged points within the twelve-mile limit, where they would rendezvous with the contact boats. This was a risky practice and required good communication, but radio helped pull it off.

The new territorial limit required Coast Guard navigators to provide sufficient proof that their seizures had taken place within the boundaries. Because this was hard to do, many rum

A letter dated March 16, 1927, from the American Consulate General in Halifax, Nova Scotia:

Subject: List of vessels seized in Nova Scotia or the other Maritime provinces for false clearance and liquor smuggling

To: The Honourable Secretary of State, Washington

An incomplete list:

Newton Bay seized on Dec. 2, 1926, charged with false clearance. Vessel placed under detention, $200 deposit.

Good Luck seized on Feb. 16, 1927, charged with false clearance, no deposit.

boat seizures ended up in court. During Prohibition, cases involving liquor violations of all types made up forty percent of all the cases before American courts. The exact location of a seizure was one of the most troublesome and important types of evidence needed in court to convict a rum-runner. The defence would often try to exploit this by offering evidence that the seizure had been made on the high seas and therefore out of Coast Guard jurisdiction.

THE CANADIAN PREVENTIVE SERVICE

Before the 1920s, the Canadian Preventive Service could do its job with a single cruiser, occasionally assisted by a few other

The rum-runner *Good Luck*, later renamed the *Apohaqui*, which was built in 1926 by W. C. McKay and Sons, Shelburne, Nova Scotia. If the weather was right, the *Good Luck* could make the run from Truro, Nova Scotia, to Bar Harbor, Maine, in eighteen hours.

vessels. But during Prohibition, Canada's anti-liquor forces were no more effective at crushing the illicit trade on water or on land than their American counterparts.

After the U.S. Coast Guard started cracking down on U.S. Prohibition laws in the mid-1920s and the Maritimes had established itself as a rum-running haven, the Preventive Service realized it had to get tough, too. It started to buy more vessels. By 1926, the service had fifteen boats, but almost all of them were purchased second-hand and were too slow and small to be effective in chasing rum-runners. But 1928, the fleet had nearly doubled in size, and between 1929 and 1931 additional modern cruisers and smaller patrol boats were added.

CGS *Adversus*, built in Orillia, Ontario, in 1931. The *Adversus* was transferred to RCMP Marine Section in 1932, stationed at Vancouver in 1933, and returned to the East Coast in 1937. It was lost in a blizzard near Shelburne, Nova Scotia, in November 1945.

On land, the police in Canada were also busy. Between 1922 and 1927, the RCMP seized more than ten thousand gallons of rum, nearly four thousand cases of assorted liquor, twenty-five automobiles, and seven vessels. But like the Canadian Preventive Service, they didn't have enough resources to stop the flow of illegal alcohol.

" I remember one particular seizure, we had good information. Well the first night we went out they didn't come in, and the second night—that would be a couple of days before Christmas, 1936. We saw the schooner come in and there were men there brought the kegs of rum ashore in dories. And they were pretty cute, too. They came up a little brook. There'd be four or five fellows and each one would have a keg of rum and they'd walk up the brook in their fishing boots, so that they didn't leave any tracks. We were very close to them. It was about two o'clock in the morning and we had on a big buffalo robe—they don't have them now. And when the job was finished we went down and declared ourselves. We arrested two of them. There was 375 five-gallon kegs in there.

Tony MacKinnon and Sgt. Churchill went back to North Sydney to arrange for a truck or one of the RCMP cutters to come and take the rum back. They took the two prisoners. And the boat arrived about six in the morning—and oh my God it was a cold night. We had to watch it all this time.

It was taken to the customs warehouse in North Sydney. It was left there till the case was disposed of in the courts. And after the court proceedings were all over we would be instructed to destroy that liquor. No, it wasn't all destroyed. But I never knew any of the RCMP fellows being dishonest with it—selling it to others. In the wintertime we would make hot toddies. When we were ordered to destroy it, we would knock out the top and spill it out into the sewer. "

—Duncan Campbell, a retired
RCMP officer in Nova Scotia

The overlap of jurisdictions and the lack of resources between the Canadian Preventive Service and the RCMP concerned the police. In 1926, Commissioner Courtland Starnes of the RCMP told a Special Commons Committee that the Preventive Service was inefficient under Customs and Excise administration and should be transferred to the RCMP. Following a major customs scandal in 1926, the Preventive Service was reorganized in 1927 and the RCMP took over trying to catch smugglers. In January 1932, for reasons of efficiency and economy, the Preventive Service became part of the RCMP.

MACHINE-GUN KELLY

CAPTAIN John Kelly of the Canadian Customs and Excise Enforcement Branch knew first-hand that trying to catch rum-

The rum-runner *Liberty*, one of the fastest rum-running boats on the East Coast

runners was neither an easy nor a safe job. While gunfire happened far less frequently in Canadian waters than in American waters, it still took place. Kelly was nicknamed "Machine-Gun Kelly" by the rum-runners because he always sailed with his machine gun on deck. Kelly used the gun to persuade rum-runners that they couldn't escape, averaging about one thousand rounds of ammunition a month.

Kelly's job was to stop smugglers bringing rum into Nova Scotia from ocean-going ships anchored offshore. The ships would anchor as far as one hundred miles offshore and transfer their cargo to smaller contact boats that stayed outside Canadian territorial waters. These boats would then bring the liquor inshore to even smaller boats that would take the alcohol to shore. Kelly had to catch boats within Canada's territorial limits. Kelly later recalled the extensive and organized operations of the rum-runners:

> It's known that the customs revenue of Canada went down between $75,000,000 and $90,000,000 within two years, due to the activities of the rum-runners.
>
> These fellows had a good organization, with mother ships out on Emerald Bank, LeHavre Bank and Roseway Bank. The contact boats like the *Muir* and the *Nashwaak*…that could carry about 800 kegs, would bring the liquor inshore to little boats that would take 80 or 100 or 120 kegs and scoot to where their hides were. All along the rock beaches and sandy beaches they would dig hides, very nice hides. On the islands they would pick out a little ravine or a valley and cut down the trees, drop the kegs and cover them over with moss and plant a few trees. If you knew your moss, you'd know it was not legitimate. You could grab a tree and pick it up. The little boats would go out to the islands. Some of the bolder ones had hides away up inshore back in the woods and on the farms.

Captain Kelly patrolled St. Margaret's Bay and other areas. Initially, he commanded a three-man crew, but this later grew to six men and finally to thirty. Each of Kelly's customs boats carried a searchlight and a machine gun, and the crews were armed with rifles. Kelly's boats may have been faster than the smugglers' rum-loaded motorboats, but the rum-runners had shortwave radios long before the Canadian Customs Force or the U.S. Coast Guard, giving them a technological advantage over the authorities, as they could send and receive coded messages from radio operators on shore, which helped them to avoid detection.

In 1929, Kelly was appointed to the *Beebe*. It was a very fast boat, thirty-eight feet long, and it fared well in summer but not as well in winter, so it was tied up at the end of December. During the summer months, Kelly would cruise around and search for rum-runners. "We were mainly of nuisance value,"

The arrow in this photo points to men loading five-gallon kegs at sea. The boats involved are the *Flora Anne* and the *Liberty*.

The *Gertrude Jean*, a rum-runner built in 1930 in Meteghan, Nova Scotia

he recalled, "but it was sufficient to pay expenses. We got one ship—the *Holly C.*—we contacted her and ran her down into the sand ledges. She struck a ledge and she sunk and that was our day's work done there. And another time there was the *Gloria P. H.* The captain saw us coming and he fired the anchor over and he got his foot in it and he went overboard too. So that was another boat picked up and she had 150 kegs aboard."

When Kelly spotted a rum-runner, he would order it to heave to. If it kept on running, as it usually did, he would use the machine gun to persuade the captain to stop. Sometimes the gunfire flew, leaving destroyed boats in its wake. In one instance, Kelly fired more than a thousand rounds at one boat, the *Gertrude Jean*. "They were all given a fair chance," Kelly later argued:

I got as close to them as the wind and water would allow and hailed and hailed them in the King's name. They'd recognize that I had seen their wheelhouse door open and I'd seen their faces in the wheelhouse windows. If it was nighttime I'd train the searchlight on them. My man Johnny—we called him "Able Seaman Splash"—was trained to run it along the water, and the spurts would be flying all up from there, and if they didn't stop we'd get right into the hull. They could see we meant business.

I remember one boat, *Gertrude Jean*, she wouldn't stop for us. She nearly rammed us, and I ran alongside for maybe two miles, and I plastered on her wind and weather, just above the water, about 1,000 or 1,500 rounds and she never came back. It ate her planks right through. She did land in St. John's, Newfoundland, but she had to be completely refitted there.

Lives were sometimes lost in the battle between authorities and rum-runners. Kelly and his crew once killed a man while intercepting a rum boat. One stormy night Kelly came across the contact boat *Newark*. It had been anchored out on LeHavre Bank and brought in about six hundred kegs and some cases of good rum. "I came upon her in the lee of Cross Island, Lunenburg County," Kelly remembered:

> There were five boats tied on the port side of her and two or three small boats on the other side and they were drifting there. One dog can only chase one cat, so one boat left and I went after that. We warned him when we went up alongside but he wouldn't stop so we had the rifles going. My machine gun fired about 40 rounds and jammed. I put it down and took a rifle, and one fellow was shot on that boat, the *Lucky Peggy*. She had 140 kegs and 20 cases of Polar Bear rum and some very choice whisky.

U.S. Coast Guard and Canadian enforcement officials couldn't end rum-running, but they were able to make thousands of arrests and seizures, greatly reducing the amount of liquor landed onshore. They also made the life of rum-runners hazardous.

" I remember searching for liquor one time and we couldn't find it anywhere, and I was leaving the place and I heard a pig in the pigpen. And I went over to have a look—I actually went over to look at the pig. There was another constable with me. And the pig was running around the pigpen and he slipped. And when he slipped he pushed the dirt aside and here was the shiny head of a spike, under about an inch of dirt in the pigpen. 'Ah,' I said, 'this is it.' So we got some boards, penned the pig up against the wall in a small area, tore up the floor, and we found the cache of rum. That happened north of Sydney.

I remember one time we searched a house and searched and searched and searched and finally we were leaving and coming outside. I looked at the floor, the step you see, and it looked odd. I got down and looked at it and I saw a little pinhole. I found a darning needle and I pressed down into this hole—the whole thing flew up. There was a spring, the board came right up—and that was the cache of rum.

Another place we were searching the water tap was where the rum came out. You turn the hot water tap and rum would come out of a big tank in the wall. They had some good caches; they were ingenious really. Then lots of times you'd come along at night and you'd stop a car and there'd be a keg in the trunk or in the backseat. There was a bootlegger in every community. Sold it out of his house, out of his barn, out of his field. Everywhere. Just as soon as we found one hide they made a better one. And there was no stigma to being a bootlegger and handling contraband rum. Everybody did it. There was nothing morally wrong....

They weren't criminals, eh? They were making a living. They were cheating the government out of some taxes that's all. "

—*William Fraser, a retired RCMP inspector in Nova Scotia.*

CHAPTER 8

THE END OF PROHIBITION

BY 1932, the backlash against Prohibition in the United States was strong. Americans were fed up. Instead of improving the nation's health and quality of life, as was intended, the experiment had ushered in one of the most crime-ridden eras in history.

The Democrats used the abolition of Prohibition as a campaign issue during the 1932 election. They won, and President Franklin Roosevelt listened to the people and, on March 23, 1933, signed into law an amendment to the Volstead Act known as the Cullen-Harrison Act, which ended Prohibition by allowing the manufacture and sale of "3.2 beer" (3.2% alcohol by weight, approximately 4% alcohol

U. S. DRINKING TO BE LEGAL FROM NOW ON

Washington Intimates Canada Will be Given Large Market For Liquor Now Stored

A headline from the December 6, 1933, edition of the *Halifax Chronicle* announcing the end of Prohibition in the United States

by volume) and light wines. The original Volstead Act had defined an "intoxicating beverage" as one with more than 0.5% alcohol. After signing the amendment, Roosevelt famously remarked, "I think this would be a good time for a beer."

By May 1933, schooners returning from Demerara in South America were clearing their rum cargoes at bargain prices; rum on the U.S. coast was going overboard for as low as $1.75 to $2 a gallon, compared to the approximately $40 commanded by rum-runners in their heyday.

This untitled traditional folk song summed up the mood of the American people during the early 1930s.

Roosevelt was elected,
Elected in time.
Went to the treasury and
found one dime.
Got back liquor
And got back beer,
Heap better times in the
next four years.

On December 5, 1933, the U.S. government repealed the Eighteenth Amendment with the ratification of the Twenty-First Amendment. The Twenty-First Amendment gave each state the right to restrict or even ban the purchase or sale of alcohol. The result was a mishmash of laws where alcohol was legally sold in some but not all towns or counties within a particular state. After the repeal of the Eighteenth Amendment, some states allowed alcohol to flow, while others continued to enforce Prohibition laws. Most states eventually chose to legalize the sale of alcohol, and in 1966, Mississippi was the last state to repeal Prohibition.

TIME TO PAY THE PIPER

On the last day of national Prohibition in the United States, the cartage operators involved in the transport of liquor to and from the dock and warehouses of St. Pierre held a "funeral parade" to commemorate the end of an era. Seventy trucks paraded throughout the community with American and French flags at half-mast.

Political events in the United States would eventually have a devastating effect on the liquor trade in St. Pierre, but in the short term, the residents of St. Pierre were expecting a windfall. Local warehousers stockpiled liquor inventories in anticipation of a flood of orders from the United States, where it was expected that the demand could not be supplied domestically. With the repeal of Prohibition, this increased demand was expected to lead to a shortage of alcohol by the end of the year. Prices were anticipated to hit the roof. St. Pierre had clearly profited during Prohibition in its legal middleman role, with some of the profits from the trade being used to improve the town by building needed infrastructure. But the big money had been made by Canadian distillers and the syndicates on the other end of the supply chain in America.

By the end of June, the share prices of liquor stocks had shot up on the stock market. For example, Walker's common stock rose from five dollars to thirty-five dollars and Consolidated Distilleries from fifty cents to nine dollars.

After the repeal of the Volstead Act, the U.S. secretary of the treasury, Henry Morgenthau, Jr., determined that Canadian distilleries owed close to sixty million dollars in evaded excise and

> " We loaded a carload of goods, got our cash, and shipped it. We shipped a lot of goods. Of course, we knew where it went, but we had no legal proof. And I never went to the other side of the border to count the empty Seagram bottles. "
>
> —*Sam Bronfman, head of the Bronfman family dynasty*

customs tariffs. Threatening a ban on legal imports from Canada until the bill was paid, the two countries negotiated a settlement. Secretary of State Cordell Hull, who handled the negotiations for the American government, eventually agreed to a settlement of five percent of the original claim. Despite being found not guilty on smuggling charges the year before, much of the cost was born by the Bronfman family of Montreal. In May of 1936, the Bronfmans, owners of the Seagram Company, agreed to pay $1.5 million to settle their account with the American treasury.

Like their American counterparts, the Canadian government was displeased with Canadian distillers like Seagram. The idea of Canadian-produced liquor being exported to St. Pierre and then returned without payment of Canadian customs and excise duties bothered Richard Bennett, who had replaced William Lyon Mackenzie King as prime minister in 1930. As the leader of the opposition, Bennett had criticized King for not acting on the recommendations a royal commission had made to proceed with prosecution of the Bronfmans for their role in the trade. Now that Bennett was in power, he was determined to launch a full investigation into the offshore smuggling business, including the "laundering" of profits earned from St. Pierre.

Late in 1934, four of the Bronfmans, their relative Barney Aaron, and sixty-five others alleged to have skilfully manipulated the government out of tax revenues were charged with "conspiring to violate the statutes of a friendly country," which

> " Prohibition in the United States sent the Americans looking for liquor in Canada, and our business prospered both with the inter-provincial business in Canada and many people from the United States coming over to Canada to buy liquor to take back with them.... "
>
> —*Harry Bronfman, Seagram Company*

RUM-RUNNING BOATS HIT THE MARKET

With Prohibition over, operators in St. Pierre and in the Maritimes wanted to get rid of their rum-running boats. The vessels were put on the market by ship brokers. The following letter dated October 25, 1934, from W. Lawrence Sweeney, a ship broker in Yarmouth, Nova Scotia, to Julien Moraze of St. Pierre, was typical:

The motor vessel *REO* is owned by Berky Cravitz, and George Morrel of Digby, Nova Scotia, is looking after her. I understand the price asked for her is $7,000. She is not a bargain at that price.

The *REO II* is under seizure at Havana, Cuba. I doubt if she will return. Harris Himmelman at Lunenburg owns the *Shogomac* which can be bought for less than $6,500. The *Beatrice L* can be bought for around $8,000. The *Shananliam* can be bought for $15,000.

There are a number of other boats here which can be bought such as the *Connoisseur*, *Ann D.*, *Apohaqui*, *Southwind*, *Placentia*, *Tatamagouche*, *Accuracy*, etc. and should any one be of interest to you I no doubt can secure full particulars from the agents of the owners.

was a cloaked way of saying smuggling, but the Crown was unable to prove this took place. The trial opened in Montreal in January 1935 and lasted until the middle of June.

On June 15 a not guilty verdict was brought down. Part of the court's judgement read, "The Crown claims that the accused opened agencies in Newfoundland and St. Pierre et Miquelon that were useless for any purpose other than smuggling, and that sales made there to Canadians constitutes proof of illegal conspiracy, yet the accused had every legal right to organize these agencies in the interests of their business.... It does not appear in the evidence that the accused did anything whatever to assist in importing liquor into Canada...and the accused are herewith discharged."

BOWING TO PRESSURE

The Canadian government was somewhat hypocritical in wanting to prosecute Canadian distillers when their own hands were far from clean. During American Prohibition, the Canadian government had received hefty tax benefits by levying a nine-dollar-per-gallon tax on all intoxicating beverages. The tax was supposed to be refunded upon presentation of a customs receipt from the country to which it was destined, but because there were no receipts from a country under Prohibition, and since most, if not all, of the liquor in question landed on American shores, these receipts were never turned over. As a result, the tax dollars piled up in Ottawa. It is estimated that the Canadian government was gathering up to thirty million dollars a year from illegal exports to the United States during the first few years of Prohibition. (This practice would eventually change after Canada bowed to American pressure.)

The French government also eventually bowed to pressure from the U.S. government. Less than two years after the end of Prohibition, France put a halt to the liquor shipping business in St. Pierre. As of April 9, 1935, shippers of alcoholic products from St. Pierre were required to post a bond guaranteeing that the goods would reach destinations shown on the manifests. For a brief time, the authorities turned a blind eye while warehouses were emptied and merchants' stocks were depleted, but stricter enforcement soon followed.

THE *KROMHOUT* INCIDENT

REPEAL of Prohibition in the United States was only hours old when a dangerous event took place in Canadian waters involving a Lunenburg-registered schooner named *Kromhout*. It illustrated the hard work of the Canadian Preventive Service and the fact that the service's work was far from over. The fate of the *Kromhout* was not unlike that of several other rum-runners caught in Canadian waters.

The *Kromhout* was about seven miles off Flint Island, near Cape Breton Island, loaded with 1,500 barrels of rum from St. Pierre, when the Preventive Service cutter *Stumble Inn*, also known as Patrol Boat Number 4, approached. Because the ship was Canadian-registered, Preventive Service officers could legally board and inspect it within the twelve-mile limit.

Milton McKenzie, a chief officer of *Stumble Inn*, recalls that the cutter approached the *Kromhout* in darkness on an early December morning in 1933. The rum-runner turned and fled. The cutter pursued. After a long chase, the *Kromhout* hove to. Captain Moyle Hyson sent a crew to take over the boat. The *Stumble Inn* headed for North Sydney with the *Kromhout* following at the end of seven hundred feet of line. Suddenly the tow line parted—it appeared that someone had cut the line. The rum-runner fled for the open sea and the police ship followed. But the *Kromhout* was a faster boat and was soon out of sight.

A huge search followed. The vessel eventually made it to port in St. Pierre. Canadian authorities had alerted the governor of St. Pierre of the incident and had asked that the vessel be held there until Canadian government officials arrived. The governor placed the ship's captain and crew in jail, and the police officers held hostage on the *Kromhout* were released. Soon the men, along with the *Kromhout*, returned to Canada.

A legal battle followed, which made it all the way to the Supreme Court. The Preventive Service proceeded with the case under Section 207 of the Customs Act, which related to hovering in territorial waters with a contraband cargo. A key piece

Patrol Boats On Watch For Craft Out Of Lunenburg

Liquor-laden Motor Vessel Kromhout Believed To Carry Four Captive Sea-going Mounties Held Prisoner When Craft Broke Away From Patrol Cutter Off Cape Breton Coast.

A headline from the December 8, 1933, edition of the *Halifax Chronicle* reporting on the search for the *Kromhout*

of evidence was a map showing the position of the *Kromhout*. Captain Ross Mason was sentenced to three years in Dorchester Penitentiary on each of three counts—theft of his own ship, theft of its liquor cargo, and resisting a police officer. The *Kromhout* was eventually sold and ended up in Bay Roberts, Newfoundland, where it served for several years as a coastal freighter.

END OF AN ERA

By the end of Prohibition, even some of its original supporters openly admitted its failure. John D. Rockefeller, a wealthy American industrialist, was one of them. He wrote in a letter in 1932,

> When Prohibition was introduced, I hoped that it would be widely supported by public opinion and the day would soon come when the evil effects of alcohol would be recognized. I have slowly and reluctantly come to believe that this has not been the result. Instead, drinking has generally increased; the speakeasy has replaced the saloon; a vast army of lawbreakers has appeared; many of our best citizens have openly ignored Prohibition; respect for the law has been greatly lessened; and crime has increased to a level never seen before.

Throughout the 1930s, law enforcement authorities in Canada and the United States kept their focus on liquor smugglers along the Atlantic coast, but by the end of the decade their attention turned to larger, more important world events. In September 1939, Germany invaded Poland and World War Two followed. As people became preoccupied with the war, the wild days of rum-running slowly began to fade and become a distant memory. Decades later, this colourful chapter of Atlantic Canadian history should neither be romanticized nor ignored. While many Maritimers saw the Prohibition era as a time when smugglers were driven by greed to break the law and exploit others' weaknesses for alcohol, the majority supported the rum-runners.

Back in the 1920s and 30s, people's sympathies were with the adventurous and enterprising rum-runners whom they saw as having an essential service to provide.

Acknowledgements

I would first like to extend special thanks to everyone at Nimbus Publishing, in particular, Dan Soucoup, Patrick Murphy, Penelope Jackson, and Caitlin Drake.

My gratitude also goes to all those before me who wrote about rum-runners and did the hard work of uncovering primary sources and materials. I owe much to the work of J. P. Andrieux and Geoff and Dorothy Robinson.

Thanks are also due to the Halifax Public Libraries, Nova Scotia Archives and Records Management, the Yarmouth County Museum and Archives, the Fisheries Museum of the Atlantic, the Maritime Museum of the Atlantic, and the Prince Edward Island Public Archives and Records Office for their wonderful collections of books, newspapers, photographs, and other materials.

Finally, thanks to my husband and best friend, Robbie Frame, for his valuable editing and unwavering support, and to my daughters, Natasha and Lara, for just being with me.

BIBLIOGRAPHY

In addition to the books and articles listed below, the following news-papers, circa 1900–2009, provided valuable research material: *Halifax Morning Chronicle, Halifax Chronicle, Lunenburg Progress-Enterprise, Charlottetown Guardian, Moncton Times, Halifax Daily Star, Nova Scotia Times, Halifax Herald, Halifax Chronicle Herald*. Some of the clippings used are contained in archival and museum holdings. Exact sources have been given in some parts of the book's text.

Andrieux, J. P. *Prohibition and St. Pierre*. Lincoln, Ontario: W. F. Rannie, 1983.

Andrieux, J. P. *Over the Side*. Lincoln, Ontario: W. F. Rannie, 1984.

Bruce, Harry. *An Illustrated History of Nova Scotia*. Halifax: Province of Nova Scotia and Nimbus Publishing, 1997.

Canney, Donald L. *Rum War: The US Coast Guard and Prohibition*. Washington: U.S. Coast Guard, 1990.

DeMont, John. "Maritime Drug Smuggling and Rum Running." *Maclean's* (May 13, 2002).

Gervais, C. H. *The Rumrunners: A Prohibition Scrapbook*. Scarborough: Firefly Books, 1980.

Hennigar, Ted. *The Rum Running Years*. Hantsport, Nova Scotia: Lancelot Press, 1981.

Marrus, Michael R. *Mr. Sam: The Life and Times of Samuel Bronfman*. New York: Viking Press, 1991.

McCarthy, A. J. *Bay of Chaleur Forgotten Treasures*. Halifax: Nimbus Publishing, 1997.

McDougall, David J. "The Origins and Growth of the Canadian Customs Preventive Service Fleet in the Maritime Provinces and Eastern Quebec, 1892–1932," *The Northern Mariner* 5, no. 4 (1995): 37–57.

McGahan, Peter. *Crime and Policing in Maritime Canada.* Fredericton: Goose Lane Editions, 1988.

Miller, Don. *I Was a Rum Runner.* Yarmouth: Lescarbot Printing, 1979.

Montague, Art. *Canada's Rumrunners.* Canmore, Alberta: Altitude Publishing Canada Ltd., 2004.

Morrison, James, and James Moreira. *Tempered by Rum: Rum in the History of the Maritime Provinces.* Porters Lake, Nova Scotia: Pottersfield Press, 1988.

Newman, Peter. *Bronfman Dynasty.* Toronto: McClelland and Stewart, 1978.

Parker, Mike. *Historic Lunenburg.* Halifax: Nimbus Publishing, 1999.

Patton, Janice. *The Sinking of the I'm Alone.* Toronto: McClelland & Stewart Limited, 1973.

Randell, Jack. *I'm Alone.* Indianapolis: The Bobbs-Merrill Company, 1930.

Robinson, Geoff. "I Want My Ship Back!" *The Atlantic Advocate* (July 1987): 41–43.

Robinson, Geoff and Dorothy Robinson. *The Nellie J. Banks.* Summerside, Prince Edward Island: Williams & Crue Ltd., 1970.

———. *Duty-Free.* Summerside, Prince Edward Island: Williams & Crue Ltd., 1992.

"Remembering Rum-Running Days." *Cape Breton Magazine* (June 1975): 1–20.

"The Rum Smugglers: Piracy, Maritime Bootlegging and Hijacking." *American Review of Reviews* 67.

Steinke, Gord. *Mobsters and Rumrunners of Canada.* Edmonton: Folklore Publishing, 2003.

Van de Water, Frederic F. *The Real McCoy.* Mystic, Connecticut: Flat Hammock Press, 2007.

Wayling, Thomas. "The Rum Patrol." *Maclean's* (October 1, 1932): 18, 33.

Willoughby, Malcolm F. *Rum War at Sea*. Washington: U.S. Government Printing Office, 1964.

IMAGE SOURCES

Page 5: Courtesy of Nova Scotia Archives and Records Management

Page 6: Photo by C. A. McBride; courtesy of Capt. Hubert Hall

Page 8: Courtesy of morgueFile

Page 12: Courtesy of Nova Scotia Archives and Records Management

Page 13: Courtesy of Sherbrooke Village

Page 14: Courtesy of Dalhousie University Archives and Special Collections; from Lucas, Rev. D. V. "The twins. A reply to the Anti-Scott Act Address of Mr. Goldwin Smith, at St. Catherines, Ont." Montreal: "Witness" Publishing House, 1885.

Page 17: Courtesy of Nova Scotia Archives and Records Management

Page 20: Courtesy of the Halifax Historical Museum, Daytona Beach, Florida

Page 22: Courtesy of the Halifax Historical Museum, Daytona Beach, Florida

Page 25: Courtesy of Hugh Corkum

Page 26: Courtesy of the Yarmouth County Museum Archives

Page 27 (top and bottom): Courtesy of the Yarmouth County Museum Archives

Page 29: Courtesy of Nova Scotia Archives and Records Management

Page 30: Courtesy of Nova Scotia Archives and Records Management

Page 34: Photo by Bob Brooks; courtesy of Hugh Corkum

Page 35: Courtesy of Hugh Corkum

Page 37: Courtesy of Hugh Corkum

Page 38: Photo by C. A. McBride; courtesy of Capt. Hubert Hall

Page 39: Photo by C. A. McBride; courtesy of Capt. Hubert Hall

Page 40 (top and bottom): Photo by C. A. McBride; courtesy of Capt. Hubert Hall

Page 41 (top and bottom): Photo by C. A. McBride; courtesy of Capt. Hubert Hall

Page 42: Photo by C. A. McBride; courtesy of Capt. Hubert Hall

Page 45: Photo by C. A. McBride; courtesy of Capt. Hubert Hall

Page 47: Courtesy of the Yarmouth County Museum Archives

Page 53: Courtesy of Trinity Historical Society Archives, Trinity, NL (RH-S1-P01)

Page 55: Courtesy of Trinity Historical Society Archives, Trinity, NL (THS-PC52)

Page 60: Courtesy of Nova Scotia Archives and Records Management

Page 61: Courtesy of Killam Memorial Library, Dalhousie University

Page 65: Courtesy of Provincial Archives New Brunswick (Leonard Violette Photo: P72-2)

Page 68: From the Nimbus archives

Page 76: Courtesy of Prince Edward Island Public Archives and Records Office

Page 77: Courtesy of Prince Edward Island Public Archives and Records Office

Page 83: Official U.S. Coast Guard photograph. Source: USCG Historian's Office

Page 84: Official U.S. Coast Guard photograph. Source: USCG Historian's Office

Page 85: Official U.S. Coast Guard photograph. Source: USCG Historian's Office

Page 86: Official U.S. Coast Guard photograph. Source: USCG Historian's Office

Page 89: Photo by C. A. McBride; courtesy of Capt. Hubert Hall

Page 90: Courtesy of Royal Canadian Mounted Police/Library and Archives Canada (PA-209445)

Page 92: Courtesy of Hugh Corkum

Page 94: Courtesy of Hugh Corkum

Page 95: Photo by C. A. McBride; courtesy of Capt. Hubert Hall

Page 99: Courtesy of Nova Scotia Archives and Records Management

Page 106: Courtesy of Nova Scotia Archives and Records Management

INDEX